# MCOLES Study Guide:

COMPREHENSIVE REVIEW WITH PRACTICE TEST QUESTIONS FOR THE MICHIGAN COMMISSION ON LAW ENFORCEMENT STANDARDS READING AND WRITING EXAM

Copyright © 2021 by Trivium Test Prep

ISBN-13: 9781637980163

ALL RIGHTS RESERVED. By purchase of this book, you have been licensed one copy for personal use only. No part of this work may be reproduced, redistributed, or used in any form or by any means without prior written permission of the publisher and copyright owner. Trivium Test Prep; Accepted, Inc.; Cirrus Test Prep; and Ascencia Test Prep are all imprints of Trivium Test Prep, LLC.

The state of Michigan was not involved in the creation or production of this product, is not in any way affiliated with Cirrus Test Prep, and does not sponsor or endorse this product. All test names (and their acronyms) are trademarks of their respective owners. This study guide is for general information and does not claim endorsement by any third party.

Image(s) used under license from Shutterstock.com

# TABLE OF CONTENTS

**INTRODUCTION** ............................................... i

**1 READING COMPREHENSION** ... 1
    Introduction ..................................1
    Topic and Main Idea .....................3
    Supporting Details ........................5
    Drawing Conclusions ....................6
    The Author's Purpose
    and Point of View .........................7
    Comparing Passages ......................9
    Meaning of Words .......................10
    Answer Key ..................................13

**2 WRITING** ... 15
    Introduction ................................15
    The Parts of Speech ....................16
    Punctuation ................................18
    Phrases ........................................19
    Clauses ........................................19
    Common Grammatical Errors .........20
    Vocabulary ..................................26
    Spelling .......................................33
    Answer Key ..................................37

**3 PRACTICE TEST ONE** ... 39
    Writing ........................................39
    Reading .......................................46
    Answer Key ..................................59

**4 PRACTICE TEST TWO** ... 67
    Writing ........................................67
    Reading .......................................74
    Answer Key ..................................85

# INTRODUCTION

Congratulations on your decision to join the field of law enforcement—few other professions are so rewarding! By purchasing this book, you've already taken the first step toward succeeding in your career. The next step is to do well on the Michigan Commission on Law Enforcement Standards (MCOLES) reading and writing tests, which will require you to demonstrate knowledge of high school–level reading and writing ability.

The Michigan Commission on Law Enforcement Standards measures test takers' writing and reading abilities to determine the likelihood of an examinee's success in law enforcement. It is the gateway for admission into the basic academy, where you will learn about police procedure and the law. The MCOLES is simply a measure of your communication skills and does not cover police procedure; that is covered in the academy.

This study guide contains a concise but comprehensive review of all sections tested on the MCOLES. It also includes two practice exams, each composed of 120 multiple-choice questions, just like the actual exam. Inside, you will also find tips, tricks, and comprehensive explanations for each testing area.

## TEST FORMAT AND STRATEGIES

The MCOLES consists of 120 questions. All the questions are multiple choice. You will have two hours to complete the exam.

MCOLES Content and Scoring

| SECTION | TOPICS | TOTAL |
|---|---|---|
| Writing | Detail<br>Spelling<br>Word Usage<br>Clarity<br>Grammar | 60 multiple-choice questions |
| Reading | Reading Comprehension | 60 multiple-choice questions |
| Total | 2 hours | 120 questions |

The test measures reading and writing aptitude. Writing questions focus on language ability. There are five question types: Detail, Spelling, Word Usage, Clarity, and Grammar. Reading questions test reading comprehension ability.

## Writing

There are five types of writing questions: Detail, Spelling, Word Usage, Clarity, and Grammar.

In DETAIL QUESTIONS, you must choose the most detailed and helpful of two statements. The questions are presented as two sentences. You will be prompted to identify and select the sentence that is most clearly and correctly written.

SPELLING QUESTIONS test your ability to spell commonly misspelled words. The questions are presented in the form of a sentence with a word missing, designated by a blank space. Keeping the sentence context in mind, you must choose the correctly spelled word option from the list of answer choices. These questions do not use words from a specific list, so you should study as many common words related to law enforcement as possible.

In WORD USAGE QUESTIONS, you must choose between two words to fill in the blank in a sentence. These questions test commonly confused words in English. You will be prompted to choose the most accurate synonym or definition, given the sentence context, from the answer choices.

CLARITY QUESTIONS provide a sentence and ask you to choose the most clearly written alternative to a phrase italicized in the sentence.

GRAMMAR QUESTIONS ask you to review a sentence that may contain a grammatical error. You then must choose if the sentence is A) correct or B) incorrect.

## Reading

The READING section of the exam contains a total of sixty multiple-choice reading comprehension questions.

Reading questions test your ability to read and understand what is being communicated in short- and moderate-length passages. The questions are presented after the passage in the form of a question stem followed by several answer choices. There will likely be multiple question stems related to one passage. You will be prompted to select answer choices based on the information contained in the passage.

Reading questions cover only common concepts. All the information needed to answer questions is contained within the passage.

# TIPS FOR TACKLING MULTIPLE-CHOICE QUESTIONS

The following tips assume you have a basic understanding of test-taking: how to follow test proctor instructions, properly record answers, make sure the answer for the right question is recorded, and review an answer sheet before submitting it. If you do nothing else to prepare, learn these quick tips. They will help you focus your efforts and use your time wisely.

## Handling Distractors

*Distractors* are the incorrect answer choices in a multiple-choice question. They distract you from the correct answer. Read and answer the following sample question:

Criminals are people who violate _____

A) Penal Code 62.

B) civil procedure.

C) martial law.

D) criminal laws.

The correct answer choice is D, criminal laws. The other incorrect answer choices—the distractors—are designed to distract the inattentive test taker by sounding right or formal. While choices A and C may be partially correct—breaking a specific penal code (criminal) or martial (civilian-imposed military) law may be a crime—neither is the *best* answer choice.

Be sure to read the question for context and tone, and try to determine what is being asked. The preceding question asked for a general definition and used wording from the question as part of the correct answer. While a criminal might violate a *specific* penal code or martial law, generally, violations can be of *any* criminal law. Because criminals are guilty of crimes and *all* criminal laws involve or pertain to crime, choice D is the *best* answer.

### Develop a Time Strategy

The examination is two hours, or 120 minutes, long. If you divide the time equally over the exam, you should have approximately one minute to answer each question. Pay attention to the time. Note the start and end time for each section prior to beginning. Make a goal to complete each question in one minute or less. One minute seems like a short amount of time, but it actually is not. You will likely complete most questions in less than thirty seconds. Develop your strategy such that you finish the easier questions quickly to allow more time to spend on the difficult questions.

Don't spend too much time on difficult questions. Mark them, skip them, and come back if you have time. If you run out of time, guess—there is no guess penalty on this exam.

### Focus on the Question

Read the question carefully. Words sometimes change meaning based on context. Context is the part of a communication that comes before or after a specific word or passage and provides clarity or meaning. Make sure you read and understand the question before selecting an answer. Read the following sentences:

> The police **ARRESTED** Chad when he was eighteen years old.
>
> Chad is thirty-two years old, but his emotional development was **ARRESTED** when he was eighteen years old.

The word *arrested* is used correctly in both sentences, but it has different meanings depending on the context.

Try to think of an answer before looking at the choices. This can keep you from being distracted by the incorrect answer choices and help you more easily identify the correct answer.

### Correct is Not Always Best

Several answers could be *correct*, or close to correct, but you must choose the *best* answer choice. Beware of answer choices that are close to the correct answer but are merely distractions.

### Use the Process of Elimination

Eliminate answer choices you know are incorrect. Choose your answer from the remaining choices.

For "all of the above" and "none of the above" answer choices, look for choices that include elements that break the "all" or "none" rule, such as a true element in a group of false elements or vice versa. If one element does not belong with the rest of the group's elements, then the answer cannot be *all*, or *none*, of the above.

Reread the question and remaining answers and select an answer choice.

# SCORING

Candidates who pass the MCOLES will receive a reported score of A, B, or C. This score is calculated by converting the raw score (the number of questions you answer correctly) into a scaled score. A score of A reflects the highest "band" of applicant scores, B reflects the middle, and C the lowest.

Test results are available online twenty-four hours after the exam. They will also be mailed to you three days after the exam. You may retake the test any time if you wish.

You must present your MCOLES Notification of Test Results form to the agency to which you are applying.

# ADMINISTRATION AND TEST DAY

The MCOLES is administered by participating law enforcement agencies and academies. To register for the exam, you must directly contact the participating agency or academy where you are applying. The MCOLES is administered online in a proctored setting. Testing sites are located throughout the state of Michigan. As of 2020, registration for the test cost sixty-eight dollars.

There is no penalty for guessing, so if you do not know the answer to a question, guess. You may get it right! Guesswork is still a matter of deduction; eliminate as many choices as possible before making a guess between the remaining answers.

On test day, arrive early. Check with the facility or participating agency to make sure you know what type of identification to bring (usually government-issued photo identification). Personal belongings, cell phones, and other electronic, photographic, recording, or listening devices are not permitted in the testing center. Many testing centers offer lockers to secure your personal items, but you should check beforehand with the facility to be sure storage is available.

You may retest any time if you wish to improve your results.

For more information or to register for a test, visit https://www.michigan.gov/mcoles/.

# About Trivium Test Prep

Trivium Test Prep uses industry professionals with decades' worth of knowledge in their fields, proven with degrees and honors in law, medicine, business, education, the military, and more, to produce high-quality test prep books for students.

Our study guides are specifically designed to increase any student's score. Our books are also shorter and more concise than typical study guides, so you can increase your score while significantly decreasing your study time.

# READING COMPREHENSION

## Introduction

In the land of movies and television, law enforcement officers are rarely shown reading. Dirty Harry, John McClane, Horatio Caine, or Andy Sipowicz would be hard-pressed to pick up the penal code, case notes, or even a newspaper! But in the real world, where shooting up the entire downtown area; costing the city and county millions of dollars in repair costs and civil suits; and turning your back on suspects to don sunglasses can get you fired, sued, or hurt, reading is a huge part of the job.

Law enforcement officers spend a considerable amount of time reading reports, case law, statutes, subpoenas, warrants, investigative notes, memos and policy changes, news reports about policing and the community, and more. Understanding what you read is paramount because it may dictate how you do the job.

You do not need to use outside knowledge on reading comprehension questions. Remember, the answer is located within the passage.

Misunderstanding what you read could cost you your job. Reading comprehension is one of the most important aspects of law enforcement. The MCOLES tests your reading comprehension abilities by presenting a passage to read, then asking several questions about the passage's content. The following information provides tips and tricks to improve your skills and navigate the reading section of the exam.

### Reading for Understanding

Reading for understanding is different from reading for entertainment. Rather than simply skimming a passage for generalized information, the reader must dig more deeply into the text, make inferences and connections, and evaluate and interpret ideas and information. However, an integral part of reading comprehension is answering questions about the information. To be proficient at comprehension, readers must master several tasks while reading a particular passage:

**Differentiate fact from opinion.** Many readers cannot tell the difference between fact and opinion. Contrary to popular belief, fact and opinion are not opposites;

instead, they are differing types of statements. A **FACT** is a statement that can be proven by direct or objective evidence. Juries are called the "finders of fact" because they use the evidence presented to prove a statement. On the other hand, an **OPINION**, though it may be based in fact, is a statement established using belief or judgment and cannot be objectively proven true or false. Opinions are not necessarily wrong; they simply are not fact.

Law enforcement officers often summarize in conversations. To ensure understanding, officers may repeat, in their own words, information a victim or suspect provides. The victim or suspect generally confirms or adjusts the restated information. To practice summarizing, after reading, take the information that is most important and restate it in your own words.

**DISTINGUISH BETWEEN WHAT IS IMPORTANT AND WHAT IS SIMPLY INTERESTING.** When determining what is important in a passage, think about the main point and tone. What is the author trying to say? What is the main point? Information that tends to strengthen or weaken the main point is important. Information that does not strengthen or weaken the main point is simply interesting.

**DETERMINE CAUSE-AND-EFFECT RELATIONSHIPS.** Determine if there is a cause-and-effect relationship between pieces of information contained in the passage. Determining cause-and-effect relationships is important in comprehension as well as in establishing potential outcomes.

Look for words that show causal relationships, like *because, since, therefore, thus,* and *so*.

**COMPARE AND CONTRAST IDEAS AND INFORMATION.** Connecting words often indicate transition within a passage. Understanding transitions can help keep you on track with the author's main point, rather than confusing you with opposing points of view in the passage. Look for words that show a shift in the author's position, such as *however, but, rather, in contrast,* and *although*.

**DRAW CONCLUSIONS.** Law enforcement officers regularly make inferences, draw conclusions, and make determinations based on information presented. After reading the passage, ask yourself:

- What judgments can be made based on the information provided?
- What evidence included in the passage supports that judgment?
- Are there other interpretations that can be made using the provided information and evidence?

## Question Types

There are seven basic types of Reading questions on the MCOLES. They are explored in more detail in the chapter.

1. **WHAT'S THE MAIN POINT?** These questions ask you to identify the author's thesis or hypothesis. A question stem relating to this question type might ask, "The passage was primarily concerned with which of the following?" Check the thesis statement or conclusion for the answer to these types of questions.

2. **WHAT'S THE SUPPORTING IDEA?** These questions generally ask you to locate specific information. A question stem relating to this question type might ask, "The passage mentions each of the following EXCEPT…" You may need to

reread the passage to find the answer. You might look for keywords in the answer choices to help steer you in the right direction.

3. **DRAWING INFERENCES.** Questions that require you to draw inferences often ask, "The passage implies which of the following?" The answer choices generally will closely imitate the text of the passage and rely upon specific facts provided.

4. **WHAT'S THE TONE?** These questions ask you to identify the author's attitude. Question stems generally ask, "The author's tone is best described as …"

5. **APPLY THE THEME TO OTHER CIRCUMSTANCES.** Questions requiring you to apply information from the passage to a similar situation often take the following form: "The author would most likely agree with which of the following?" There is no shortcut or trick to answering these question types. The key is identifying the heart of the passage and relating it to similar answer choices.

6. **LOGICAL REASONING.** This question style is the reverse of the "Application" question style. Logical reasoning questions ask you to take information from *outside* the passage and apply it to the passage to make determinations. An example of a logical reasoning question might be "Which of the following, if true, would most weaken the main point of the second paragraph?" Understanding the author's main point or argument and using your reasoning abilities to determine the value of answer choices will help you answer these questions.

7. **RELATING DIFFERENT IDEAS.** These questions require you to determine the relationship between different ideas or parts of the passage. Questions are framed in a variety of ways, but they might ask how two paragraphs relate to each other or how an idea in one sentence contrasts with an idea later in the passage.

> ⚠ Read the passage carefully. Do not skim the passage. Read it two or three times to ensure you understand what the passage is communicating. Remember, reading questions check comprehension. Reading too quickly can cause you to miss important information.

> ⚠ Read the passage before the questions. Reading the questions first can distract you from the main point of the passage. An error is more likely if you answer the question prematurely and without full understanding.

## TOPIC AND MAIN IDEA

The **TOPIC** is a word or short phrase that explains what a passage is about. The **MAIN IDEA** is a complete sentence that explains what the author is trying to say about the topic. Generally, the **TOPIC SENTENCE** is the first (or near the first) sentence in a paragraph. It is a general statement that introduces the topic so the reader knows what to expect.

The **SUMMARY SENTENCE**, on the other hand, frequently (but not always!) comes at the end of a paragraph or passage because it wraps up all the ideas presented. This sentence summarizes what an author has said about the topic. Some passages, particularly short ones, will not include a summary sentence.

> ✓ To find the main idea, identify the topic and then ask, *What is the author trying to tell me about the topic?*

Table 1.1. Identifying Topic and Main Idea

Noise complaints are one of the most common calls received by police officers in cities and suburban areas. Close quarters and strong personalities make it more likely that neighbors will butt heads; the officer's job is to keep the peace. Usually, an officer can solve the problem by warning the offender. Most people will immediately turn down their music or end a late-night party when they find out they risk a hefty fine. On rare occasions, officers will issue citations for violating city ordinances or will arrest offenders for crimes like disorderly conduct.

| TOPIC SENTENCE | Noise complaints are one of the most common calls received by police officers in cities and suburban areas. |
|---|---|
| TOPIC | noise complaints |
| SUMMARY SENTENCE | Close quarters and strong personalities make it more likely that neighbors will butt heads; the officer's job is to keep the peace. |
| MAIN IDEA | Officers respond to noise complaints, which are very common in crowded areas, to restore order. |

### Examples

1. **Topic**

   Police dogs usually work from six to nine years. K-9 officers have a variety of professional responsibilities: sniffing out explosives and narcotics, finding missing persons and human remains, and protecting officers. Many of them retire to live a comfortable life with their handlers, who know them better than anyone.

   What is the topic of the passage?

   A) dog lifespan

   B) police dogs

   C) dog handlers

2. **Main Idea**

   The Battle of the Little Bighorn, commonly called Custer's Last Stand, was a battle between the Seventh Cavalry Regiment of the US Army and the combined forces of the Lakota, the Northern Cheyenne, and the Arapaho tribes. Led by war leaders Crazy Horse and Chief Gall and religious leader Sitting Bull, the allied tribes of the Plains Indians decisively defeated their US foes. Two hundred and sixty-eight US soldiers were killed, including Lieutenant Colonel George Armstrong Custer, two of his brothers, his nephew, his brother-in-law, and six Indian scouts.

   What is the main idea of this passage?

   A) Most of Custer's family died in the Battle of the Little Bighorn.

   B) The Seventh Cavalry Regiment was formed to fight Native American tribes.

   C) The Battle of the Little Bighorn was a significant victory for the Plains Indians.

# SUPPORTING DETAILS

Statements that describe or explain the main idea are **SUPPORTING DETAILS**. Supporting details are often found after the topic sentence. They support the main idea through examples, descriptions, and explanations.

Authors may add details to support their argument or claim. **FACTS** are details that point to truths, while **OPINIONS** are based on personal beliefs or judgments. To differentiate between fact and opinion, look for statements that express feelings, attitudes, or beliefs that cannot be proven (opinions) and statements that can be proven (facts).

> ⚠ To find supporting details, look for sentences that connect to the main idea and tell more about it.

Table 1.2. Supporting Details and Fact and Opinion

Police academies have strict physical requirements for cadets. Cadets must pass fitness tests and train daily. As a result, some new recruits worry about their physical fitness before heading into the academy. Some graduates suggest focusing on core strength. Others believe that boxing is the best workout. We feel that cardiovascular activity is the most important exercise.

| | |
|---|---|
| **SUPPORTING DETAILS** | Cadets must pass fitness tests and train daily. |
| **FACT** | Police academies have strict physical requirements for cadets. |
| **OPINION** | We feel that cardiovascular activity is the most important exercise. |

### Examples

3. **Supporting Details**

   Increasingly, companies are turning to subcontracting services rather than hiring full-time employees. This provides companies with advantages like greater flexibility, reduced legal responsibility to employees, and lower possibility of unionization within the company. However, this has led to increasing confusion and uncertainty over the legal definition of employment. Courts have grappled with questions about the hiring company's responsibility in maintaining fair labor practices. Companies argue that they delegate that authorlty to subcontractors, while unions and other worker advocate groups argue that companies still have a legal obligation to the workers who contribute to their business.

   Which detail BEST supports the idea that contracting employees is beneficial to companies?

   A) Uncertainty over the legal definition of employment increases.

   B) Companies still have a legal obligation to contractors.

   C) There is a lower possibility of unionization within the company.

4. **Fact and Opinion**

   An officer cited a motorist for reckless driving. The driver was performing unsafe maneuvers. The motorist was "doing donuts," rotating the vehicle. The officer observed this activity in a parking lot after dark. The officer wrote a citation. In addition, the vehicle was impounded.

   Which statement from the passage is an opinion?

   A) An officer cited a motorist for reckless driving.

   B) The driver was performing unsafe maneuvers.

   C) The motorist was "doing donuts," rotating the vehicle.

# Drawing Conclusions

Look for facts, character actions and dialogue, how each sentence connects to the topic, and the author's reasoning for an argument when drawing conclusions.

Readers can use information that is EXPLICIT, or clearly stated, along with information that is IMPLICIT, or indirect, to make inferences and DRAW CONCLUSIONS. Readers can determine meaning from what is implied by using details, context clues, and prior knowledge. When answering questions, consider what is known from personal experiences and make note of all information the author has provided before drawing a conclusion.

Table 1.3. Drawing Conclusions

When the Spanish-American War broke out in 1898, the US Army was small and understaffed. President William McKinley called for 1,250 volunteers to serve in the First US Volunteer Cavalry. The ranks were quickly filled by cowboys, gold prospectors, hunters, gamblers, Native Americans, veterans, police officers, and college students looking for an adventure. The officer corps was composed of veterans of previous wars. With more volunteers than it could accept, the army set high standards: all the recruits had to be skilled on horseback and with guns. Consequently, they became known as the Rough Riders.

| QUESTION | Why are the volunteers named Rough Riders? |
|---|---|
| EXPLICIT INFORMATION | Different people volunteered, men were looking for adventure, recruits had to be extremely skilled on horseback and with guns due to a glut of volunteers. |
| IMPLICIT INFORMATION | Men had previous occupations; officer corps veterans worked with volunteers. |
| CONCLUSION DRAWN | The men were called Rough Riders because they were inexperienced yet enthusiastic to help with the war and were willing to put in extra effort to join. |

### Example

5. **Drawing Conclusions**

   "Swatting" is a dangerous practice. Someone falsely reports a crime in progress at a location to attract a large number of police to the site. The false crime usually involves hostages or a similar violent scenario, so police are prepared for confrontation. In fact, the term swatting is derived from the name for those police who specialize in such situations: the SWAT team, which carries high-caliber weapons and deploys flash bangs and tear gas. In a swatting incident, innocent citizens are shocked by a sudden police raid on their home. Likewise, police ready to face a violent perpetrator are surprised to find a family eating dinner or watching TV. The confusion caused by the false information and urgency of the raid make it very dangerous for all involved. Tragic outcomes are not uncommon.

   Which conclusion about the effects of swatting is most likely true?

   A) Swatting is increasingly common, thanks to social media.
   B) Swatting mostly occurs where there are large SWAT teams.
   C) Swatting can result in injury or death to innocent citizens or officers.

# THE AUTHOR'S PURPOSE AND POINT OF VIEW

The **AUTHOR'S PURPOSE** is his or her reason for writing a text. Authors may write to share an experience, to entertain, to persuade, or to inform readers. This can be done through persuasive, expository, and narrative writing.

**PERSUASIVE WRITING** influences the actions and thoughts of readers. Authors state an opinion, then provide reasons that support the opinion. **EXPOSITORY WRITING** outlines and explains steps in a process. Authors focus on a sequence of events. **NARRATIVE WRITING** tells a story. Authors include a setting, plot, characters, problem, and solution in the text.

Use the acronym P.I.E.S.—*persuade, inform, entertain, state*—to help you remember elements of an author's purpose.

Authors also share their **POINT OF VIEW** (perspectives, attitudes, and beliefs) with readers. Identify the author's point of view by word choice, details, descriptions, and characters' actions. The author's attitude, or **TONE**, can be found in word choice that conveys feelings or stance on a topic.

**TEXT STRUCTURE** is the way the author organizes a text. A text can be organized to show problem and solution, to compare and contrast, or even to show cause and effect. Structure of a text can give insight into an author's purpose and point of view. If a text is organized to pose an argument or advertise a product, it can be considered persuasive. The author's point of view will be revealed in how thoughts and opinions are expressed in the text.

Table 1.4. The Author's Purpose and Point of View

Officer ride-alongs are a great way for community members to get to know law enforcement officers. They are a valuable opportunity for students, journalists, community leaders, and those considering a career in law enforcement to learn more about the day-to-day experiences of police business. In a ride-along, you join an officer as he or she responds to calls, stops cars, and interacts with the public. Riders can ask questions and see the world from the perspective of a cop. Ride-alongs are a wonderful way for members of the public to learn about policing.

| | |
|---|---|
| **AUTHOR'S PURPOSE** | persuade readers of the benefit of ride-alongs |
| **POINT OF VIEW** | advocates ride-alongs as "a great way for community members to get to know law enforcement officers" |
| **TONE** | positive, encouraging, pointing out the benefits of ride-alongs, using positive words like *great* and *wonderful* |
| **STRUCTURE** | descriptive: describes ride-alongs, giving specific examples to support the argument that they are valuable |

## Examples

6. **Author's Purpose**

    Several law enforcement departments in the United States have implemented sUAS (small unmanned aircraft systems), or drone programs. Drones provide intelligence, surveillance, and reconnaissance, known as ISR, helping inform decision-makers in reconstructing accidents and crime scenes, finding victims in search and rescue, and managing fire scenes. Local jurisdictions, such as the Los Angeles County Sheriff's Department, use drones. So do federal agencies like the US Border Patrol. What was once a military tool is becoming a valuable resource for law enforcement.

What is the purpose of this passage?

- **A)** to argue that drones are important for patrol
- **B)** to explain the history of drones in law enforcement
- **C)** to describe how drones are used by law enforcement agencies

7. **Point of View**

Any law enforcement officer should expect to use force on the job at some point. Fortunately, officers have many nonlethal options for controlling a suspect or situation. Tasers, pepper spray, and batons are all effective for neutralizing a threat in many circumstances. Officers also train in basic ground and hand-to-hand tactics, though if possible they should avoid physical encounters for safety reasons. However, in certain situations officers must use their service pistols, which may result in a fatality.

Which of the following BEST describes what the author believes?

- **A)** Most forms of nonlethal force are effective, but not all.
- **B)** Lethal force should never be used because it is unethical.
- **C)** Officers should use nonlethal force if possible.

8. **Tone**

Managing people is complicated in any field, and law enforcement is no different. Managers must balance administrative, financial, disciplinary, and policy responsibilities. Good managers also need to be aware of their subordinates' mental health in stressful fields like law enforcement. Recognizing the signs of stress, depression, substance abuse, and afflictions like post-traumatic stress disorder (PTSD) is an important skill for those who manage law enforcement personnel. The department can provide officers with support for mental wellness, improving their job performance and safety. The sooner a supervisor can spot symptoms, the faster the officer can receive assistance.

Which of the following best describes the author's attitude toward officers' mental health?

- **A)** dismissive
- **B)** sympathetic
- **C)** pitying

9. **Text Structure**

Increasingly, police departments require law enforcement officers to wear body cameras when they interact with members of the public. Some officers agree with this policy because the cameras provide protection against false complaints of police misconduct. Footage can exonerate police officers, proving their professionalism in situations. Other officers are cautious, worried that the cameras could limit officer discretion. Their concern is that supervisors might review and second-guess the officers' decisions during a call. What is undeniable is that the trend of body cameras is not going away as more jurisdictions across America adopt them.

What is the structure of this text?

- A) cause and effect
- B) order and sequence
- C) compare and contrast

## COMPARING PASSAGES

Sometimes readers need to compare and contrast two texts. Such questions are not common on the MCOLES, but it is good to be prepared for them. After reading and identifying the main idea of each text, look for similarities and differences in the main idea, details, claims, evidence, characters, and so on.

When answering questions about two texts, first identify whether the question is about a similarity or a difference. Then look for specific details in the text that connect to the answers. After that, determine which answer choice best describes the similarity or difference.

> ⚠ Use a Venn diagram, table, or highlighters to organize similarities and differences between texts.

Table 1.5. Comparing Passages

**INTRANASALLY ADMINISTERED NALOXONE**

Because even tiny amounts of the dangerous narcotic Fentanyl can result in overdose or death, many law enforcement officers carry the anti-overdose drug naloxone in case they encounter the frequently abused substance. Naloxone can be administered intranasally, allowing for rapid absorption into the bloodstream. The rescuer lays the victim on his or her back and sprays the medication into one nostril. The rescuer needs minimal training to administer naloxone in this way.

**INJECTABLE NALOXONE**

Naloxone, a medication that counteracts opioid overdose, is carried by many law enforcement officers in case of accidental contact with powerful narcotics like Fentanyl. Naloxone must be injected by trained first responders. Injectable naloxone is effective when the nasal cavity is damaged, for instance, if the victim has head trauma. Injectable naloxone is also used on detection dogs that have accidentally inhaled Fentanyl or another opioid and need a lower dose of naloxone than a human would.

| | |
|---|---|
| **SIMILARITIES (COMPARISON)** | Both substances are used by law enforcement to fight accidental opioid overdose. |
| **DIFFERENCES (CONTRAST)** | Intranasally administered naloxone works rapidly and can be given by anyone. Injectable naloxone must be administered by a trained first responder and is more effective in specific situations. |

### Example

10. **Comparing Passages**

    <u>Self-Driving Cars: A Safer America</u>

    Self-driving cars, already present on our streets, are the wave of the future. They will make roads safer. Unlike human drivers, self-driving cars don't drink and drive, get lost in conversation, or fumble with phones. They can also be programmed to strictly adhere to the speed limit and traffic laws. That makes them the best bet for road and highway safety. Law enforcement officials will have more time to pursue violent criminals if they don't need to spend as much time monitoring highways for speeders and unsafe drivers.

<u>The Dangers of Autonomous Vehicles</u>

Many people are excited about autonomous vehicles, or self-driving cars, but they are risky machines. Already, several have been involved in deadly accidents, failing to brake for pedestrians or making inappropriate turns resulting in wrecks. Autonomous vehicles can malfunction; they occupy a gray area for law enforcement. What if an autonomous vehicle is speeding? How can highway patrol pull it over? What is the role for the traffic officer in an accident caused by a self-driving car? Who is accountable? There is no substitution for an experienced human driver with good judgment.

Which of these statements BEST compares the information in both texts?

**A)** Autonomous vehicles are a social advantage.

**B)** People are already using self-driving cars.

**C)** Self-driving cars occupy a legal gray area.

## MEANING OF WORDS

To understand the meanings of unfamiliar words, use **CONTEXT CLUES**. Context clues are hints the author provides to help readers define difficult words. They can be found in words or phrases in the same sentence or in a neighboring sentence. Look for synonyms, antonyms, definitions, examples, and explanations in the text to determine the meaning of the unfamiliar word.

Sometimes parts of a word can make its meaning easier to determine. **AFFIXES** are added to **ROOT WORDS** (a word's basic form) to modify meaning. **PREFIXES** are added to the beginning of root words, while **SUFFIXES** are added to the ending. Divide words into parts, finding meaning in each part. Take, for example, the word *unjustifiable*: the prefix is *un–* (*not*), the root word is *justify* ("to prove reasonable"), and the suffix is *–able* (referring to a quality). Affixes are discussed in more detail in chapter 2.

> ⚠ Use what you know about a word to figure out its meaning, then look for clues in the sentence or paragraph.

Another way to determine the meaning of unknown words is to consider their denotation and connotation with other words in the sentence. **DENOTATION** is the literal meaning of a word, while **CONNOTATION** is the positive or negative associations of a word.

Authors use words to convey thoughts, but the meaning may be different from a literal meaning of the words. This is called **FIGURATIVE LANGUAGE**. Types of figurative language include similes, metaphors, hyperboles, and personification.

Similes compare two things that are not alike with the words *like* or *as*. Metaphors are used to compare two things that are not exactly alike but may share a certain characteristic.

Hyperboles are statements that exaggerate something to make a point or to draw attention to a certain feature. Personification involves using human characteristics to describe an animal or object.

Table 1.6. Meanings of Words

Check fraud used to be a major crime, but today fewer people than ever use paper checks. Still, criminals continue to find ways to steal from consumers. Identity theft is a threat to all Americans as more people use credit cards and electronic financial applications than cash. Despite encryption techniques that protect personal details, computer hackers periodically uncover consumers' financial information in security breaches. Small-time thieves steal credit cards, use card skimmers at gas stations, or make fake cards with specialized machines.

| | |
|---|---|
| **CONTEXT CLUES** | Techniques *protect* personal details; the details are still *uncovered* for criminal use. |
| **AFFIXES** | The prefix *en–* in *encryption* means *cause to*. The suffix *–ion* suggests an act or process. |
| **ROOTS** | The root of the word *encryption* is *crypt*, which means *hide* or *conceal*. |
| **MEANING** | *Encryption* means "the process of causing something to be hidden." |

## Examples

11. **Context Clues**

    After a few high-profile missing-persons cases in the 1970s and 1980s, parents in many communities became concerned about "stranger danger." Families worried that their children would be abducted, taken by criminal outsiders. However, when a child goes missing, the perpetrator is usually someone the child knows. Family members make up the majority of perpetrators in cases of missing children. It is very rare that a child is kidnapped by a total stranger, though it can happen.

    What does *abducted* mean as it is used in the passage?

    A) taken by criminal outsiders

    B) the perpetrator

    C) family members make up

12. **Root Words and Affixes**

    Unfortunately, automobile accidents happen. The good news is, most result in only minor damage to vehicles. Still, drivers are responsible for calling the police and reporting the incident, regardless of its severity. An officer will arrive to take the statement of each driver and survey the scene. The officer will closely examine the drivers' behavior and mannerisms to determine if their claims are credible. After all the evidence is collected, reviewed, and approved, the insurance company assigns blame to one party. The officer's role is key in this determination.

    Based on affixes and context clues, what does *credible* mean?

    A) believable

    B) achievable

    C) likeable

13. **Figurative Language**

    Nothing in the world is harder than waking up for a job you don't love. Who wants to drag themselves to work every day? That's why it's important to follow your passions. Many say that serving the public in law enforcement is more than just a job; it's a calling. Police officers risk their lives to serve and protect the public. It takes a certain kind of person to thrive in law enforcement.

    Which type of figurative language is used in the second sentence?

    **A)** simile

    **B)** metaphor

    **C)** personification

# Answer Key

1. **B) Correct.** The topic of the passage is police dogs. The passage mentions how long they work, their handlers, and the usual retirement circumstances of police dogs as supporting ideas.

2. **C) Correct.** The author writes that "the allied tribes…decisively defeated their US foes," and the remainder of the passage provides details to support this idea.

3. **C) Correct.** The passage specifically presents this detail as one of the advantages of subcontracting services.

4. **B) Correct.** The statement "The driver was performing unsafe maneuvers" is a judgment about the safety of the actions taken by the driver. The driver (or his attorney) might argue that his driving was safe.

5. **C) Correct.** The passage states that swatting is dangerous because of confusion caused by false information and the nature of a violent raid. The sentence "Tragic outcomes are not uncommon" suggests that injury or death can happen.

6. **C) Correct.** The text provides details on how drones are used and what departments use them.

7. **C) Correct.** The author discusses many options for nonlethal force, using the word *fortunately* to show a preference for it. However, the author also allows that lethal force is sometimes necessary.

8. **B) Correct.** The author states that "[t]he department can provide officers with support" and that supervisors should "be aware of their subordinates' mental health." By taking these positions, the author is being sympathetic and supportive of officers' mental health.

9. **C) Correct.** In this text, two perspectives on body cameras are compared and contrasted.

10. **B) Correct.** Both passages indicate that self-driving cars, or autonomous vehicles, are already in use.

11. **A) Correct.** The phrase "taken by criminal outsiders" redefines the word *abducted* in the sentence.

12. **A) Correct.** The root *cred* means *believe*. The words *evidence*, *reviewed*, and *approved* are context clues hinting that something needs to be believed and accepted.

13. **B) Correct.** The writer uses the metaphor *drag*. No one literally drags himself or herself to work.

**READING COMPREHENSION** 13

# WRITING

## INTRODUCTION

Written and verbal communications are equally important in law enforcement. Writing accurate, clear, and concise memos, warrants, and police reports ensures that the information provided is as the officer intended. Unclear or confusing verbal communication can create misunderstanding and even danger if an officer is attempting to control a volatile situation. The same is true of written work. Wordy, incoherent, error-laden communications create confusion.

The MCOLES tests five aspects of writing: detail, spelling, word usage, clarity, and grammar.

Clear and concise writing helps readers easily understand a message. In law enforcement, the last thing an officer wishes is for lawyers, juries, or the public to have to *guess* what he or she meant in a report or other written communication. Cases have been won and lost based on officer testimony related to a well-written or poorly written report.

Inspect the following two passages as an example of how wordiness and grammatical errors can confuse communication.

> **PASSAGE ONE**
>
> On Friday, August 17, 2014, about 1530 hours while working as a patrol officer in full uniform in Sector 2 of River City I heard over my car radio that Officer Smith had two people in front of Superior Court with warrants. I arrived at the Superior Court and met with Officer Smith. Officer Smith told me a woman, identified as Jane Johnson, and a man, identified as Ronald Jones, were at the courthouse. Jane and Ronald were at the court for a family hearing.
>
> A records check with River City Records and Warrants confirmed Jane had a misdemeanor warrant, and Ronald had a felony warrant, out of River City.
>
> Jane and Ronald were arrested without incident to answer for the warrant.

> **PASSAGE TWO**
>
> On Friday, August 17, 2014, about 1530 hours I contacted Jane Johnson and Ronald Jones in front of the River City Superior Court. Jane and Ronald were at the court for a family hearing. I had information both parties had active warrants for their arrest.
>
> A records check with River City Records and Warrants confirmed Jane had an active misdemeanor warrant for her arrest and Ronald had an active felony warrant for his arrest, both issued by River City.
>
> I arrested Jane and Ronald without incident to answer for their warrants.

Isn't it much easier to understand passage two? Are the sentences clear, concise, and grammatically correct, and do they contain all the necessary information? On the other hand, does passage one seem wordy and filled with grammatical errors? Is it clear or confusing? Unclear reports of search warrants could lead to poor investigations, arrests, and prosecutions.

On Clarity and Grammar questions, the MCOLES will test common grammatical mistakes. Knowing the rules of grammar, mechanics, and sentence structure will help you succeed. Furthermore, avoiding common errors can help add clarity to your written communication. We review the basics and common mistakes in this chapter.

On Spelling and Word Usage questions, the MCOLES will also ask you to properly use and spell words. Two sections of this chapter focus on building your vocabulary, determining the meaning of unfamiliar words, and reviewing spelling rules.

## THE PARTS OF SPEECH

**NOUNS** are the words that describe people, places, things, and ideas. The subject of a sentence is typically a noun. For example, in the sentence "The station was very clean," the subject, *station*, is a noun; it is a place.

Nouns have several subcategories: common nouns (*chair, car, house*), proper nouns (*Julie, David*), noncountable nouns (*money, water*), and countable nouns (*dollars, cubes*), among others. There is much crossover among these subcategories (for example, *chair* is both common and countable), and other subcategories do exist.

> ⚠️
> **SINGULAR PRONOUNS**
> • I, me, my, mine
> • you, your, yours
> • he, him, his
> • she, her, hers
> • it, its
> **PLURAL PRONOUNS**
> • we, us, our, ours
> • they, them, their, theirs

**PRONOUNS** replace nouns in a sentence or paragraph, allowing a writer to achieve a smooth flow throughout a text by avoiding unnecessary repetition. While there are countless nouns in the English language, there are only a few types of pronouns. Take the sentence "Sam stayed home from school because Sam was not feeling well." The noun *Sam* appears twice in the same sentence. Instead, the pronoun *he* can be used to stand in for *Sam*: "Sam stayed home from school because he was not feeling well."

**VERBS** express action (*run, jump, play*) or state of being (*is, seems*). Verbs that describe action are **ACTION VERBS**, and those that describe being are **LINKING VERBS**.

ACTION: My brother <u>plays</u> tennis.

LINKING: He <u>is</u> the best player on the team.

**ADJECTIVES** provide more information about a noun in a sentence. Take the sentence "The boy hit the ball." If you want your readers to know more about the noun *boy*, you could use an adjective to describe him: *the little boy, the young boy, the tall boy.*

**ADVERBS** describe verbs, adjectives, and even other adverbs. For example, in the sentence "The doctor had recently hired a new employee," the adverb *recently* tells us more about how the action *hired* took place.

> ⚠ Participles are nouns or adjectives formed by adding *–ed* or *–ing* to a verb.
> <u>Seated</u> politely, Ron listened to his friend's boring story.
> Maya petted the <u>sleeping</u> cat.

**PREPOSITIONS** express the location of a noun or pronoun in relation to other words and phrases described in a sentence. For example, in the sentence "The nurse parked her car in a parking garage," the preposition *in* describes the position of the car in relation to the garage. Together, the preposition and the noun that follow it are called a **PREPOSITIONAL PHRASE**. In this example, the prepositional phrase is *in a parking garage.*

**CONJUNCTIONS** connect words, phrases, and clauses. **INTERJECTIONS**, like *wow* and *hey*, express emotion and are most commonly used in conversation and casual writing.

### Examples

1. Which of the following lists includes all the nouns in the following sentence?

    I have lived in Minnesota since August, but I still don't own a warm coat or gloves.

    **A)** coat, gloves

    **B)** I, coat, gloves

    **C)** Minnesota, August, coat, gloves

2. Which of the following lists includes all the adjectives in the following sentence?

    The new chef carefully stirred the boiling soup and then lowered the heat.

    **A)** new, boiling

    **B)** new, carefully, boiling

    **C)** new, carefully, boiling, heat

3. Choose the word that best completes the sentence.

    Her love _____ blueberry muffins kept her coming back to the bakery every week.

    **A)** to

    **B)** with

    **C)** of

# PUNCTUATION

The basic rules for using the major punctuation marks are given in the table below.

Table 2.1. Using Punctuation

| PUNCTUATION | PURPOSE | EXAMPLE |
| --- | --- | --- |
| Period | Ending sentences | Periods go at the end of complete sentences. |
| Question mark | Ending questions | What's the best way to end a sentence? |
| Exclamation point | Ending sentences that show extreme emotion | I'll never understand how to use commas! |
| Comma | Joining two independent clauses (always with a coordinating conjunction) | Commas can be used to join clauses, but they must always be followed by a coordinating conjunction. |
| | Setting apart introductory and nonessential words and phrases | Commas, when used properly, set apart extra information in a sentence. |
| | Separating items in a list | My favorite punctuation marks include the colon, semicolon, and period. |
| Semicolon | Joining together two independent clauses (never used with a conjunction) | I love exclamation points; they make sentences seem so exciting! |
| Colon | Introducing a list, explanation, or definition | When I see a colon, I know what to expect: more information. |
| Apostrophe | Forming contractions | It's amazing how many people can't use apostrophes correctly. |
| | Showing possession | Parentheses are my sister's favorite punctuation; she finds commas' rules confusing. |
| Quotation marks | Indicating a direct quote | I said to her, "Tell me more about parentheses." |

## Examples

4. Which of the following sentences contains an error in punctuation?
    A) I love apple pie! John exclaimed with a smile.
    B) Jennifer loves Adam's new haircut.
    C) Billy went to the store; he bought bread, milk, and cheese.

5. Which punctuation mark correctly completes the following sentence?
Sam, do you want to come with us for dinner_
    A) .
    B) ?
    C) ;

## PHRASES

Understanding subjects and predicates is key to understanding what a phrase is. The **SUBJECT** is what the sentence is about; the **PREDICATE** contains the verb and its modifiers.

> The nurse at the front desk will answer any questions you have.
> **SUBJECT:** the nurse at the front desk
> **PREDICATE:** will answer any questions you have

A **PHRASE** is a group of words that communicates only part of an idea because it lacks either a subject or a predicate. Phrases can begin with prepositions, verbs, nouns, or participles.

> **PREPOSITIONAL PHRASE:** The dog is hiding <u>under the porch</u>.
> **VERB PHRASE:** The chef <u>wanted to cook</u> a different dish.
> **NOUN PHRASE:** <u>The big red barn</u> rests beside <u>the vacant chicken house</u>.
> **PARTICIPIAL PHRASE:** <u>Walking quietly</u>, she tried not to wake the baby.

### Example

6. Identify the type of phrase underlined in the following sentence:

    The experienced paraprofessional worked independently <u>with the eager students</u>.

    A) prepositional phrase
    B) noun phrase
    C) verb phrase

## CLAUSES

**CLAUSES** contain both a subject and a predicate. They can be either independent or dependent. An **INDEPENDENT** (or main) **CLAUSE** can stand alone as its own sentence.

> The dog ate her homework.

**DEPENDENT** (or subordinate) **CLAUSES** cannot stand alone as their own sentences. They start with a subordinating conjunction, relative pronoun, or relative adjective, which will make them sound incomplete.

> <u>Because</u> the dog ate her homework

Clauses can be joined together to create more complex sentences. **COORDINATING CONJUNCTIONS** join two independent clauses, and **SUBORDINATING CONJUNCTIONS** join an independent to a dependent clause.

Table 2.2. Conjunctions

| | | |
|---|---|---|
| **Coordinating** | for, and, nor, but, or, yet, so (FANBOYS) | The nurse prepared the patient for surgery, <u>and</u> the doctor performed the surgery. |
| **Subordinating** | after, although, because, if, since, so that, though, until, when, while | She had to ride the subway <u>because</u> her car was being serviced. |

### Example

7. Choose the word that best completes the sentence.

    Christine left her house early on Monday morning, _____ she was still late for work.

    A) but

    B) and

    C) for

## COMMON GRAMMATICAL ERRORS

### Pronoun-Antecedent Agreement

Pronouns must agree with their ANTECEDENTS (the words they replace) in number; however, some pronouns also require gender agreement (*him, her*). PRONOUN-ANTECEDENT AGREEMENT rules can be found below:

1. Antecedents joined by *and* typically require a plural pronoun.
   The <u>children and their dogs</u> enjoyed <u>their</u> day at the beach.
   If the two nouns refer to the same person, a singular pronoun is preferable.
   <u>My best friend and confidant</u> still lives in <u>her</u> log cabin.

2. For compound antecedents joined by *or*, the pronoun agrees with the nearer or nearest antecedent.
   Either the resident mice <u>or the manager's cat</u> gets <u>itself</u> a meal of good leftovers.

3. When indefinite pronouns function in a sentence, the pronoun must agree with the number of the indefinite pronoun.
   <u>Neither</u> student finished <u>his or her</u> assignment.
   <u>Both</u> students finished <u>their</u> assignments.

4. When collective nouns function as antecedents, the pronoun choice will be singular or plural depending on the function of the collective.
   The <u>audience</u> was cheering as <u>it</u> rose to <u>its</u> feet in unison.
   Our <u>family</u> are spending <u>their</u> vacations in Maine, Hawaii, and Rome.

5. When *each* and *every* precede the antecedent, the pronoun agreement will be singular.
   <u>Each and every man, woman, and child</u> brings unique qualities to <u>his or her</u> family.
   <u>Every creative writer, technical writer, and research writer</u> is attending <u>his or her</u> assigned lecture.

How would you complete the following sentence? "Every boy and girl should check _____ homework before turning it in." Many people would use the pronoun *their*. But since the antecedent is "every boy and girl," technically, the correct answer would be *his or her*. Using *they* or *their* in similar situations is increasingly accepted in formal speech, however. It is unlikely that you will see questions like this on a police exam, but if you do, it is safest to use the technically correct response.

> **Example**
>
> 8. In which of the following sentences do the nouns and pronouns NOT agree?
>    A) After we walked inside, we took off our hats and shoes and hung them in the closet.
>    B) The members of the band should leave her instruments in the rehearsal room.
>    C) The janitor on duty should rinse out his or her mop before leaving for the day.

**Vague or Unclear Pronouns**

A vague or unclear reference is generally the result of a **PRONOUN ERROR**. Pronoun errors occur when it is not clear what the antecedent of a pronoun is—the word it replaces. In the first sentence below, it is difficult to determine whose notes the officer gave to the Assistant District Attorney. Do the notes belong to the officer or to the ADA? The antecedent of the pronoun *his* is unclear. To improve this sentence, be sure the pronoun refers to only one antecedent noun.

> **WRONG**: Officer Lane gave Assistant District Attorney Poole his notes.
>
> **CORRECT**: Officer Lane gave his notes to Assistant District Attorney Poole.

Another way to ensure clarity in writing is to avoid using pronouns to refer to an implied idea; it is better to state the idea explicitly. In the sentence below, the writer misuses the pronoun *it*. The reader might be confused: did jury deliberation take a long time, or did the process of the trial take a long time? To improve this sentence, the writer should state the idea explicitly, avoiding a pronoun altogether.

> **WRONG**: The jury reached a verdict in the defendant's case, but it took a long time.
>
> **CORRECT**: The jury reached a verdict in the defendant's case, but the deliberations took a long time.

> **Example**
>
> 9. Read the following sentence and decide whether it is grammatically correct or incorrect.
>
>    John said he and Frank were fighting when he was shot.
>
>    A) Correct
>    B) Incorrect

**Subject-Verb Agreement**

Verbs are conjugated to indicate **PERSON**, which refers to the point of view of the sentence. First person is the speaker (*I, we*); second person is the person being addressed (*you*); and third person is outside the conversation (*they, them*). Verbs are also conjugated to match the NUMBER (singular or plural) of their subject. HELPING VERBS (*to be, to have, to do*) are used to conjugate verbs. An unconjugated verb is called an INFINITIVE and includes the word *to* in front of it (*to be, to break*).

Table 2.3. Verb Conjugation (Present Tense)

| PERSON | SINGULAR | PLURAL |
| --- | --- | --- |
| First person | I give | we give |
| Second person | you give | you (all) give |
| Third person | he/she/it gives | they give |

> Ignore words between the subject and the verb when trying to match a subject and verb:
> The new library ~~with its many books and rooms~~ fills a long-felt need.

Verbs must agree in number with their subjects. (In some other languages, such as Spanish, verbs must also agree with their subjects in gender.) SUBJECT-VERB AGREEMENT rules follow:

1. Singular subjects agree with singular verbs; plural subjects agree with plural verbs.
   The girl walks her dog.
   The girls walk their dogs.

2. Compound subjects joined by *and* typically take a plural verb unless they are considered one item.
   Correctness and precision are required for all good writing.
   Macaroni and cheese makes a great snack for children.

3. Compound subjects joined by *or* or *nor* agree with the nearer or nearest subject.
   Neither I nor my friends are looking forward to our final exams.
   Neither my friends nor I am looking forward to our final exams.

4. All singular indefinite pronouns agree with singular verbs.
   Neither of the students is happy about the play.
   Each of the many cars is on the grass.
   Every one of the administrators speaks highly of Officer Larkin.

5. All plural indefinite pronouns agree with plural verbs.
   Several of the students are happy about the play.
   Both of the cars are on the grass.
   Many of the administrators speak highly of Officer Larkin.

6. Some of the singular indefinite pronouns (*all, most, some, more, any*) change agreement depending on the object of the preposition.
   All of the pie is gone.
   All of the pies are gone.
   Some of the bucket is dirty.
   Some of the buckets are dirty.

7. Collective nouns agree with singular verbs when the collective acts as one unit. Collective nouns agree with plural verbs when the collective acts as individuals within the group.
   The jury announces its decision after sequestration. (*They act as one unit.*)
   The jury make phone calls during their break time. (*They act as individuals.*)

8. Nouns that are plural in form but singular in meaning will agree with singular verbs.
   Measles is a painful disease.
   Sixty dollars is too much to pay for that book.
9. Singular verbs come after titles, business corporations, and words used as terms.
   "Three Little Kittens" is a favorite nursery rhyme for many children.
   General Motors is a major employer for the city.

### Example

10. Read the following sentence and decide whether it is grammatically correct or incorrect.
    Some of the officers at the station is planning to stay late.
    A) Correct
    B) Incorrect

## Verb Tense Agreement

Verbs are also conjugated to indicate TENSE, or when the action has happened. Actions can happen in the past, present, or future. Tense also describes over how long a period the action took place.

- **SIMPLE** verbs describe general truths or something that happened once.
- **CONTINUOUS** verbs describe an ongoing action.
- **PERFECT** verbs describe repeated actions or actions that started in the past and have been completed.
- **PERFECT CONTINUOUS** verbs describe actions that started in the past and are continuing.

Table 2.4. Verb Tenses

| TENSE | PAST | PRESENT | FUTURE |
| --- | --- | --- | --- |
| Simple | I gave her a gift yesterday. | I give her a gift every day. | I will give her a gift on her birthday. |
| Continuous | I was giving her a gift when you got here. | I am giving her a gift; come in! | I will be giving her a gift at dinner. |
| Perfect | I had given her a gift before you got there. | I have given her a gift already. | I will have given her a gift by midnight. |
| Perfect continuous | Her friends had been giving her gifts all night when I arrived. | I have been giving her gifts every year for nine years. | I will have been giving her gifts on holidays for ten years next year. |

The verb tenses in a sentence must agree with each other and with the other information provided in the sentence. Pay attention to words like *before, after, tomorrow, yesterday, then,* and *next*, which describe when in time events occurred.

**WRONG:** After he changed clothes, the officer will be ready to go home.
**CORRECT:** After he changed clothes, the officer was ready to go home.

In the example above, the introductory phrase describes an action that was completed in the past (*he changed*), so the rest of the sentence should also be in the past (*was ready*).

### Example

11. Which verb phrase best completes the sentence?

    By this time tomorrow, we _____ in New York.
    A) will have arrived
    B) have arrived
    C) arrive

## Comparing Adjectives and Adverbs

The suffix *–er* is used when comparing two things, and the suffix *–est* is used when comparing more than two. Adjectives longer than two syllables are compared using *more* (for two things) or *most* (for three or more things).

> Anne is taller than Steve, but Steve is more coordinated.
>
> Of the five brothers, Billy is the funniest, and Alex is the most intelligent.

*More* and *most* should NOT be used in conjunction with *–er* and *–est* endings.

> **Wrong:** My most warmest sweater is made of wool.
>
> **Correct:** My warmest sweater is made of wool.

### Example

12. Which of the following sentences contains an adjective error?
    A) The new red car was faster than the old blue car.
    B) Reggie's apartment is in the tallest building on the block.
    C) Of the four speeches, Jerry's was the most long.

## Misplaced Modifiers

A **modifier** is a word or phrase—like an adjective—that adds detail to a sentence. Adjectives, adverbs, and modifying phrases should be placed as close as possible to the word they modify. **Misplaced modifiers** can create confusing or nonsensical sentences. On the MCOLES, they may appear in Grammar or Clarity questions.

> **Wrong:** Running down the alley, the siren sounded and the police officer knew backup had arrived.
>
> **Correct:** Running down the alley, the police officer heard the siren and knew backup had arrived.

In the first example above, the phrase "running down the alley" looks like it is modifying "the siren." For clarity, it should be placed next to "the police officer," the noun it modifies.

> **Wrong:** Describing the crime, the jury listened to the prosecutor deliver his opening statement.

> **CORRECT:** The jury listened to the prosecutor deliver his opening statement describing the crime.

In this example, the phrase "describing the crime" is first placed next to the word "jury," making it seem like the jury is describing the crime. To fix the sentence, the modifier should be moved so it is clear that the prosecutor is describing the crime.

### Example

13. Choose the more clearly written sentence.
    A) During police contacts, failure to follow directions is often the cause of officer uses of force.
    B) During police contacts, failure to follow directions often is the cause of officer uses of force.

## Sentence Fragments

A sentence fragment occurs when a group of words is followed by a period but does not form a complete sentence or thought. A sentence fragment can be corrected by turning it into a complete sentence that has at least one independent clause. Look out for sentence fragments on Grammar or Clarity questions.

> **WRONG:** Because he was tired of presiding over cases involving the same criminals in his courtroom.
>
> **CORRECT:** The judge left the bench because he was tired of presiding over cases involving the same criminals in his courtroom.

### Example

14. Choose the more clearly written sentence.
    A) The suspect robbed an elderly woman and then fled the scene in a red sedan heading northbound on Eighth Avenue.
    B) The suspect robbed an elderly woman and then fled the scene in a red sedan. Heading northbound on Eighth Avenue.

## Run-on Sentences

A **run-on sentence** is two or more complete sentences not separated by appropriate punctuation, such as a comma, period, or semicolon. For example, the following is a run-on sentence: "Jack shot his friend Mark over a pool game, Jack was mad because he thought Mark was cheating."

Be sure to separate each complete thought with proper punctuation. Applying this rule changes the preceding sentence: "Jack shot his friend Mark over a pool game. Jack was mad because he thought Mark was cheating."

### Example

15. Choose the more clearly written sentence.
    A) Jane broke into the house intending to steal items to exchange for drugs she activated the alarm and ran away.
    B) Jane broke into the house intending to steal items to exchange for drugs. She activated the alarm and ran away.

# Vocabulary

Vocabulary is a collection of words used or known in language. Possessing a large vocabulary can help you better understand communications. It can improve your ability to determine context and add clarity to the written or spoken word. Law enforcement vocabulary can be very technical, but it also contains many commonly used words. The MCOLES will test your vocabulary on **Word Usage** questions, which measure your ability to understand and appropriately use *common* words. You may also encounter homophones, or words that sound the same but are spelled differently and have different meanings. These and other commonly confused words are covered later in the section.

Developing a large vocabulary takes time and practice; it cannot be done overnight. However, studying commonly used words and their synonyms can help. Synonyms are words that share the same or nearly the same meaning as other words. Understanding word roots, prefixes, suffixes, and how they affect words can also help you determine the meaning of unfamiliar words based on the word's structure.

## Root Words

A ROOT WORD is the base of a word. It comes after a prefix or before a suffix. In English, many root words come from ancient Greek and Latin. Root words hold meaning and can stand alone as words. Learning to recognize common root words can help you build your vocabulary and make educated guesses about unfamiliar words. It can also help improve your ability to comprehend various types of communications.

Table 2.5 lists some common root words, their meanings, and examples.

Table 2.5. Common Root Words

| ROOT | MEANING | EXAMPLES |
| --- | --- | --- |
| *actus, act* | drive, lead, act | active, action, activate, react |
| *acurer* | to sharpen | acute, acumen, acuity |
| *agon* | contest, struggle | antagonist, agony |
| *ambi* | both | ambiguous, ambidextrous |
| *anthropo* | man, human, humanity | anthropologist, philanthropist |
| *aqua* | water | aquarium, aquatic |
| *arbit* | judge | arbitrary, arbitration |
| *archos, arch* | chief, first, rule | monarch, archangel, anarchy |
| *aud* | to hear | audience, audible, auditory |
| *auto* | self | autobiography, autograph, autoimmune, automobile |
| *bene* | good | benevolent, beneficial |
| *bio* | life | biology, biography |
| *capere, cip, cept* | take, seize | captive, capture, captivate, intercept |
| *cedere, ced* | to go, yield | recede, precede, exceed, predecessor |
| *chron* | time | chronological, chronic, synchronize |
| *circum* | around | circumference, circumvent, circumscribe |

| ROOT | MEANING | EXAMPLES |
| --- | --- | --- |
| clino, clin | lean, slant | incline, decline, inclination, recline |
| contra, counter | against | contradict, contrary, counteract |
| cred | believe | creed, incredible |
| crit | judge | criticize, critical |
| crypto, crypt | hide, conceal | cryptic, cryptogram, encryption |
| dict | to say | dictation, dictate, predict |
| duc, duct | to lead | conduct, induce, induct |
| dyna | power | dynamic, dynamite, dynamo |
| dys | bad, hard, unlucky | dysfunctional, dyslexic, dystopia |
| equ | equal, even | equidistant, inequity, equivalent, equitable |
| errare, err, errat | wander, go astray | errant, err, erratic, aberration |
| fac | to do, to make | factory, manufacture, artifact |
| finis, fin | end, limit | final, definite, infinite |
| form | shape | conform, reform |
| fort | strength | fortitude, fortress, fortify, comfort |
| fract | to break | fracture, fraction |
| gno, gnos | know | diagnosis, ignore, incognito, cognitive |
| gram | something written | telegram, diagram, grammar |
| graph | writing | graphic, autograph |
| gravis, grav, griev | heavy, serious | grave, grievance, grievous, aggravate, gravity |
| hetero | different | heteronym, heterogeneous |
| homo | same | homonym, homogenous |
| hydro | water | hydrate, dehydrate, hydraulic |
| hypo | below, beneath | hypothermia, hypothetical, hypoglycemic |
| ject | throw | eject, project, reject |
| jud | judge | judicial, prejudice |
| jus, jur, just | right, law, oath | abjure, perjury, conjure, jury, jurisprudence |
| juven | young | juvenile, rejuvenate |
| mal | bad | malfeasance, malevolent, malcontent |
| mater | mother | maternal, maternity |
| meter, metr | measure | thermometer, perimeter, metric |
| micro | small | microbe, microscope, microchip |
| mis, miso | hate, wrong | misanthrope, misogyny, misbehave |
| mono | one | monologue, monotonous, monotheism |
| morph | form, shape | morphology, metamorphosis |
| mort | death | mortal, mortician, immortal |
| multi | many | multimedia, multiple, multiply, multicolored |
| nym | name | antonym, synonym, homonym |

**WRITING** 27

Table 2.5. Common Root Words (continued)

| ROOT | MEANING | EXAMPLES |
| --- | --- | --- |
| onus, oner | burden | onerous, onus, exonerate |
| opsis, optic | sight, eye, view | optical, synopsis |
| pater | father | paternal, paternity |
| phil | love | philanthropist, philosophy |
| phobia | fear | claustrophobia, acrophobia, phobic |
| phon | sound | cacophony, phonetic, symphony |
| photo, phos | light | photograph, photogenic, phosphorous |
| placaere | appease | placate, placid |
| port | to carry | portable, transportation, export |
| pretiare, prec | to value | precious, deprecation, depreciation, appreciation |
| pseudo | false | pseudonym, pseudoscience |
| psycho | soul, spirit | psychology, psychic, psychotic |
| rupt | to break | bankrupt, disrupt, erupt |
| scope | to watch, see | microscope, telescope |
| scrib, scribe | to write | inscribe, prescribe, describe |
| sect, sec | to cut | bisect, section, intersect, dissect |
| sentire, sent | to feel, perceive | consent, resent, sentient, sentiment |
| skep, scop | examine | skeptical, scope |
| spect | to look | inspect, spectator, circumspect, retrospective |
| struct | to build | construct, destruct, restructure, infrastructure |
| tacere, tac, tic | to be silent | tacit, taciturn, reticent |
| techno | art, science, skill | technique, technology |
| tele | far off | television, telephone, teleport |
| tendere | stretch | extend, tend, distend |
| terrere, terr | frighten | deter, terror, terrorism |
| therm | heat | thermal, thermometer, thermos |
| thesis | position | synthesis, hypothesis |
| venire, veni, ven | come, move toward | convention, contravene, intervene |
| vid, vis | to see | video, envision, evident, vision |
| voc | to call | voice, vocalize, advocate |
| zelos | ardor | zeal, zealous, zealot |

## Prefixes

PREFIXES are sets of letters that are added to the beginning of a word. Adding a prefix to a word can change its meaning. For instance, if you take the root word *jud*, which means *judge*, and add the prefix *pre–*, which means *before*, you create the word *prejudice*, which means to prejudge.

Prefixes cannot stand on their own as words, but they do hold meaning. Learning to recognize common prefixes builds vocabulary and helps readers make educated guesses about unfamiliar words. It can also help improve reading comprehension in general.

Table 2.6 lists some common prefixes, their meanings, and examples.

Table 2.6. Common Prefixes

| PREFIX | MEANING | EXAMPLES |
| --- | --- | --- |
| *ambi–, amb–* | around, on both sides | ambiguous, ambivalent |
| *anti–* | against, opposite | anticlimactic, antiseptic |
| *bi–* | two | bicycle, bifocals, bilingual |
| *circum–, circa–* | around, about | circumference, circadian, circumvent |
| *com–, con–* | with | communicate, convince |
| *contra–* | against | contradict, contrary, contravene |
| *de–* | reduce, remove | devalue, decelerate, decompose |
| *di, dis–* | not, opposite of | discontinue, disappear, discover, digress |
| *en–, em–* | cause to, into | enact, empower, embrace, enclose |
| *fore–* | before, front of | foreshadow, forebear |
| *il–, im–, in–, ir–* | not, without | illegal, impossible, invalidate, irresponsible |
| *im–, in–* | in, into | import, income |
| *inter–* | between, among | interrupt, intercept, intercede |
| *mid–* | middle | midterm, midway |
| *mis–* | bad, wrong | misinterpret, misspell |
| *non–* | not, without | nonconformist, nonfiction, nonviolent |
| *over–* | excessive | overeat, overconfident |
| *peri–* | around, about | perimeter, periphery |
| *pre–* | before | preexisting, precedent, preview |
| *re–, red–* | again, back, against, behind | recede, redo, retreat, rewrite |
| *semi–* | half, partial | semiconscious, semicircle |
| *sub–* | under | subway, submarine |
| *super–* | above, beyond | superfluous, superhuman, superior |
| *trans–* | across, over, through, beyond | transmit, transgression, transit |
| *un–* | not, opposite of | unusual, unashamed, unfair |

### Suffixes

**Suffixes** are the same as prefixes except that suffixes are added to the ends of words rather than the beginnings.

Table 2.7 lists some common suffixes, their meanings, and examples.

Table 2.7. Common Suffixes

| SUFFIX | MEANING | EXAMPLES |
| --- | --- | --- |
| –able, –ible | is, can be | excitable, moveable, collectible |
| –al, –ial | having characteristics of, pertaining to | facial, procedural, universal |
| –cide, –cidum | kill | homicide, insecticide |
| –ed | past tense | arrested, called, treated |
| –en | made of, to cause to be | awaken, frighten, weaken |
| –er, –or | a person who | pioneer, professor, volunteer |
| –er | more | taller, meaner, shorter |
| –est | the most | fastest, meanest, shortest |
| –ful | full of | helpful, shameful, thankful |
| –ic | relating to, having characteristics of | poetic, dogmatic, organic |
| –ing | present participles, materials | sleeping, eating, bedding, frosting |
| –ion, –tion, –ation, –sion | act, process | submission, celebration, navigation |
| –ity, –cy –ty | state of, condition | activity, civility, normalcy, society |
| –ive, –ative, –itive | quality of | active, qualitative, sensitive |
| –ize | to make (forms verb) | compartmentalize, mechanize |
| –less | without | blameless, homeless, remorseless |
| –ly | in the manner of | bravely, courageously, horrifically |
| –ment | state of being, act of | contentment, placement, resentment |
| –ness | state of, condition of | weakness, kindness |
| –ology | study | biology, physiology, sociology |
| –ous, –eous, –ious | having qualities of, full of | riotous, hazardous, righteous, gracious |
| –y | characterized by | sassy, cheeky, slimy |

## Homophones

Homophones are words that sound alike but are spelled differently and hold different meanings, such as *break* and *brake*.

> Officer Brady stepped on the brake to stop the car.
> Officer Brady took a lunch break during his shift.

Commonly confused words include:

- **ACCEPT**: agree
  **EXCEPT**: not including
- **ALOUD**: said out loud
  **ALLOWED**: able to
- **BARE**: uncovered
  **BEAR**: large animal; to carry
- **BRAKE**: to stop
  **BREAK**: to damage or interrupt
- **DIE**: to no longer be alive
  **DYE**: to artificially change color
- **EFFECT**: result (noun)
  **AFFECT**: to change (verb)
- **FLOUR**: used for cooking
  **FLOWER**: grows out of the ground
- **HEAL**: to get better
  **HEEL**: the back part of the foot
- **HOLE**: an opening
  **WHOLE**: all of something
- **INSURE**: to have insurance (*I need to insure my car.*)
  **ENSURE**: to make sure something happens (*She ensured that the dog found a good home.*)
- **MEAT**: the flesh of an animal
  **MEET**: to see someone
- **MORNING**: the start of the day
  **MOURNING**: grieving
- **PATIENCE**: tolerating annoyances
  **PATIENTS**: people receiving medical care
- **PEACE**: not at war
  **PIECE**: a part of something
- **POOR**: having very little money
  **POUR**: to dispense from a container
- **PRINCIPAL**: the leader or administrative head of a school
  **PRINCIPLE**: a strongly held belief
- **RAIN**: precipitation
  **REIN**: a strap that controls an animal
  **REIGN**: to rule over
- **RIGHT**: correct; a legal entitlement
  **RITE**: a ritual
  **WRITE**: to put words on paper
- **STAIR**: used to get from one floor to another
  **STARE**: a long, fixed look
- **SUITE**: a set of rooms
  **SWEET**: the taste associated with sugar; pleasant, nice, kind
- **THEIR**: belonging to them (*they brought their luggage*)
  **THERE**: a place (*the luggage is over there*)
  **THEY'RE**: they are (*they're looking for the luggage*)
- **THROUGH**: to go in one side and out the other
  **THREW**: tossed (past tense of *throw*)
- **TO**: the preposition indicating movement or purpose (*I am going to work to do my job.*)
  **TOO**: in addition (*I'm coming too.*)
  **TWO**: more than one; dual (*two officers patrol this area together*)
- **WEAR**: to put on (*I'll wear my new dress.*)
  **WHERE**: to question about place (*Where is the door?*)
- **YOUR**: belonging to you (*your car*)
  **YOU'RE**: you are (*you're going to need a new car*)

## Commonly Confused Words

Some words are similar in meaning, but are not synonyms. However, they are commonly confused in writing and speech. A hallmark of good writing is the proper use of these words.

Table 2.8 contains some commonly confused words.

Table 2.8. Commonly Confused Words

| CONFUSED WORDS | DEFINITION |
|---|---|
| Amount | describes a noncountable quantity (*an unknown amount of jewelry was stolen*) |
| Number | describes a countable quantity (*an unknown number of necklaces was stolen*) |
| Bring | toward the speaker (*bring to me*) |
| Take | away from the speaker (*take away from me*) |
| Farther | a measurable distance (*the house farther up the road*) |
| Further | more or greater (*explain further what you mean*) |
| Fewer | a smaller amount of something plural (*fewer chairs*) |
| Less | a smaller amount of something that cannot be counted (*less water*) |
| Lose | to fail to win; to not be able to find something (*to lose a game; to lose one's keys*) |
| Loose | relaxed; not firmly in place (*my pants are loose*) |

### Examples

*In the following questions, select the best word to complete the sentence from the two choices.*

16. The officer notified the suspect of his _____.
    - **A)** rites
    - **B)** rights

17. We took a _____ before the evening shift.
    - **A)** break
    - **B)** brake

18. Because of his _____ the victim testified against the criminal.
    - **A)** principals
    - **B)** principles

19. Everyone said the victim was a _____ lady.
    - **A)** sweet
    - **B)** suite

20. We ran out of gas and could not drive any _____ down the road.
    - **A)** further
    - **B)** farther

# SPELLING

Why is spelling important in law enforcement? Much of what officers write is by hand, at least initially. What's more, any notes or other material an officer writes in connection with a crime or criminal investigation is *discoverable*. That means the court can compel an officer to turn over his or her notes and communications to the court and lawyers for both sides. Right or wrong, spelling could affect the officer's credibility and competence in the eyes of a jury. Many people believe multiple spelling and grammatical errors show a lack of attention to detail and a tendency toward sloppy work. Both are detrimental to effective police work.

The MCOLES does test on spelling. Thankfully, spelling is the easiest part of the examination to study for. And while you could relegate yourself to simply repetitively writing random words on a piece of paper like you did after school when you were in trouble with the teacher, there are more focused methods to improve your performance on a multiple-choice spelling test. It can help to learn the following tips, tricks, and rules to prevent common spelling errors.

## Special Spelling Rules

*i* comes before *e* except after *c*

Generally, the letter *i* comes before the letter *e* in a word except when the *i* is preceded by the letter *c*.

- p<u>ie</u>ce
- sal<u>ie</u>nt
- <u>cei</u>ling
- con<u>cei</u>vable

> ⚠ Be cautious of the rule "*i* comes before *e* except after *c*," for it has many exceptions: "Your foreign neighbors weighed the iciest beige glaciers!"

There are some notable exceptions where the letter e comes before the letter i, such as:

- words that end in *cie*, like *proficient* or *ancient*
- plural words ending in *–cies*, like *policies*
- words with an *ay* sound, like *eight*, *vein*, or *neighbor*

When adding a suffix to a word, change the final *y* to an *i*.

- lazy → laziest
- tidy → tidily

For words that end with the letters *–le*, replace the letter *e* with the letter *y*: subtle → subtly

## Plurals

Regular nouns are made plural by adding *s*. Irregular nouns can follow many different rules for pluralization, which are summarized in the following table.

Table 2.9. Irregular Plural Nouns

| ENDS WITH... | MAKE IT PLURAL BY... | EXAMPLE |
| --- | --- | --- |
| y | changing y to i and adding –es | baby → babies |
| f | changing f to v and adding –es | leaf → leaves |
| fe | changing f to v and adding –s | knife → knives |
| o | adding –es | potato → potatoes |
| us | changing –us to –i | nucleus → nuclei |

| ALWAYS THE SAME | DOESN'T FOLLOW THE RULES |
| --- | --- |
| sheep | man → men |
| deer | child → children |
| fish | person → people |
| moose | tooth → teeth |
| pants | goose → geese |
| binoculars | mouse → mice |
| scissors | ox → oxen |

Pluralize words ending in –ch, –s, –sh, –x, or –z by adding –es to the end.

- catch → catches
- pass → passes
- push → pushes
- annex → annexes
- blitz → blitzes

An exception to the –ch rule includes words where the ch makes a k sound. For those words, simply add the letter s to the end of the word: stomach → stomachs.

## Possessives Versus Contractions

A **contraction** is a combination of two words that is shortened by using an apostrophe to indicate the missing letter or letters. For instance, *cannot* is shortened to *can't*; the apostrophe stands in for the missing letters *n* and *o*.

A **possessive** is a word with an apostrophe added to indicate possession. For example, rather than writing "the duty belt that belongs to Pat," write "Pat's duty belt."

A notable exception to this rule—and a common mistake—is the improper use of the contraction *it's* as a possessive, *its*.

The contraction for *it is* or *it has* is *it's*: "It's dangerous in that area of town at night."

The word *its* is possessive and shows ownership of the pronoun *it*, such as "the jury reached *its* verdict" or "the suspect's car was badly damaged, and *its* license plate was obscured."

### Conjugating Verbs

The suffixes *–ed* or *–ing* added to a regular verb generally signify the verb's tense. For example, the present tense of the verb *to question* is *question*. ("You question the suspect while I write the report.")

To show that the event happened in the past (or to form the past tense), the word *question* becomes *questioned*. And to refer to an action that is still happening (or to form the present participle), *question* becomes *questioning*. (See above for more details on conjugating verbs.)

There are some exceptions to the general rules for conjugating regular verbs.

For verbs ending with a silent *–e*, drop the *–e* before adding *–ed* or *–ing*.

- fake → faked → faking
- ache → ached → aching

When verbs end in the letters *–ee*, do not drop the second *e*. Instead, simply add *–d* or *–ing*.

- free → freed → freeing
- agree → agreed → agreeing

When the verb ends with a single vowel plus a consonant, and the stress is at the end of the word, then the consonant must be doubled before adding *–ed* or *–ing*.

- commit → committed → committing
- refer → referred → referring

If the stress is not at the end of the word, then the consonant can remain singular.

- target → targeted → targeting
- visit → visited → visiting

Verbs that end with the letter *c* must have the letter *k* added before receiving a suffix: panic → panicked → panicking

### Examples

*Read the following sentences and choose the correct spelling of the missing word.*

21. The defendant asked the court to show him _____ in the punishment for his crime.
    - A) lienency
    - B) leniency
    - C) leneincy

22. Deputy Smith found _____ in the inmate's cell.
    - A) contriband
    - B) controband
    - C) contraband

WRITING

23. Evidence that is fleeting or that can fade away over time is said to be of an _____ nature.
    A) effervescent
    B) evanecent
    C) evanescent

24. Officer Jones attempted to _____ the victim's blood loss by applying pressure to the wound.
    A) mitagate
    B) mitegate
    C) mitigate

# Answer Key

1. **C) Correct.** *Minnesota* and *August* are proper nouns, and *coat* and *gloves* are common nouns. *I* is a pronoun, and *warm* is an adjective that modifies coat.

2. **A) Correct.** *New* modifies the noun *chef*, and *boiling* modifies the noun *soup*.
   B) Incorrect. *Carefully* is an adverb modifying the verb *stirred*.
   C) Incorrect. *Heat* is a noun.

3. A) Incorrect. *To* frequently indicates position; it does not make sense here.
   B) Incorrect. *With* often implies a physical connection; it does not make sense here.
   **C) Correct.** The correct preposition is *of*. The preposition *of* usually shows a relationship and may accompany a verb.

4. **A) Correct.** Choice A should use quotation marks to set off a direct quote: *"I love apple pie!" John exclaimed with a smile*.

5. **B) Correct.** The sentence is a question, so it should end with a question mark.

6. **A) Correct.** The phrase is a prepositional phrase beginning with the preposition *with*. The preposition *with* modifies *the eager students*.

7. **A) Correct.** In this sentence, the conjunction is joining together two contrasting ideas, so the correct answer is *but*.

8. A) Incorrect. In this sentence, *hats* and *shoes* and *them* are all plural; they agree.
   **B) Correct.** *The members of the band* is plural (*members*), so it should be replaced by the plural pronoun *their* instead of the singular *her*.
   C) Incorrect. *Janitor* is singular, so the singular pronouns *his or her* are correct.

9. **B) Correct.** This sentence is grammatically incorrect. The sentence contains a vague reference; it is unclear who was shot.

10. **B) Correct.** This sentence is grammatically incorrect. It contains a verb error; the verb *is* should be plural: *are*. All plural indefinite pronouns agree with plural verbs. Here, the subject of the sentence, *some*, is a plural indefinite pronoun, so it requires a plural verb.

11. **A) Correct.** The phrase *by this time tomorrow* describes an action that will take place and be completed in the future, so the future perfect tense (*will have arrived*) should be used.

12. **C) Correct.** This sentence should read, "Of the four speeches, Jerry's was the longest." The word *long* has only one syllable, so it should be modified with the suffix *–est*, not the word *most*.

WRITING 37

13. **A)** **Correct.** Choice B has a misplaced modifier (the word *often*).

14. **A)** **Correct.** Choice B contains a sentence fragment.

15. **B)** **Correct.** Choice A is a run-on sentence.

16. A) Incorrect. A *rite* is a ritual.
    **B)** **Correct.** *Rights* refers to a legal entitlement.

17. **A)** **Correct.** A *break* is a brief interruption, in this context, for rest.
    B) Incorrect. To *brake* means to stop, usually a vehicle in motion.

18. A) Incorrect. A *principal* is the administrative head of a school.
    **B)** **Correct.** *Principles* are strongly-held beliefs.

19. **A)** **Correct.** *Sweet* means kind or caring.
    B) Incorrect. A *suite* is a set of rooms.

20. **B)** **Correct.** *Farther* refers to a measurable distance—in this case, a distance of road.

21. **B)** **Correct.** *Leniency* is the correct spelling.

22. **C)** **Correct.** *Contraband* is the correct spelling.

23. **C)** **Correct.** *Evanescent* is the correct spelling.

24. **C)** **Correct.** *Mitigate* is the correct spelling.

# PRACTICE TEST ONE

## Writing

### Grammar

Read the sentence, decide whether it is grammatically correct or incorrect, then choose the correct answer.

1. In addition to the disastrous effects an active volcano can have on it's immediate surroundings, an eruption can also pose a threat to passing aircraft.
   - A) Correct
   - B) Incorrect

2. Most of the grass has lost their deep color.
   - A) Correct
   - B) Incorrect

3. The grandchildren and their cousins enjoyed their day at the beach.
   - A) Correct
   - B) Incorrect

4. The employer decided that he could not, due to the high cost of health care, afford to offer no other benefits to his employees.
   - A) Correct
   - B) Incorrect

5. Although Puerto Rico is known for it's beaches, its landscape also includes mountains, which are home to many of the island's rural villages.
   - A) Correct
   - B) Incorrect

6. Engineers design seat belts to stop the inertia of traveling bodies by applying an opposing force on the driver and passengers during a collision.
   - A) Correct
   - B) Incorrect

7. Because of its distance from the sun, the planet Neptune has seasons that last the equivalent of forty-one Earth years.
   - A) Correct
   - B) Incorrect

8. Animals use estivation to avoid harsh conditions and to help it survive winter.
   - A) Correct
   - B) Incorrect

9. Andy Warhol's paintings, in addition to being the subject of the largest single-artist museum in the United States, are in great demand.

    A) Correct
    B) Incorrect

10. The Iris and B. Gerald Cantor Roof Garden, atop the Metropolitan Museum of Art in New York City, offer a remarkable view.

    A) Correct
    B) Incorrect

**Clarity**

Read the sentence, then review the alternatives to the portion that is italicized. Choose the one that fits the sentence's context and is most clearly stated.

11. Marge told Ruth that *Marge's supervisor wanted to speak with Ruth.*

    A) Marge's supervisor wanted to speak with Ruth.
    B) her supervisor wanted to speak with her.
    C) her supervisor was desiring to speak with Ruth.

12. Inmates received lunches *in bags from deputies*.

    A) in bags from deputies.
    B) from deputies in bags.
    C) to be distributed by deputies in bags.

13. Officers *who train rarely are caught off guard*.

    A) Officers who train rarely are caught off guard.
    B) Officers that train rarely are caught off guard.
    C) Officers who train are rarely caught off guard.

14. Fran was very afraid, *but she kept it hidden*.

    A) but she kept her fear hidden.
    B) but she kept it hidden.
    C) and so she kept that hidden.

15. Someone stole the packages *left at the door by the delivery driver*.

    A) left at the door by the delivery driver.
    B) at the door left by the delivery driver.
    C) by the delivery driver left at the door.

16. Community policing is not a new concept, *but it has, however, recently received a face-lift*.

    A) being that it has, however, recently received a face-lift.
    B) but it has, however, recently received a face-lift.
    C) but it has recently received a face-lift.

17. Every time Alonzo turned on the TV, *the news reported another city was experiencing unrest*.

    A) they said another city was experiencing unrest.
    B) the news reported another city was experiencing unrest.
    C) it was reported that another city was experiencing unrest.

18. My aunt and uncle, who live in Wyoming, *had made plans to visit us over the holidays*.

    A) had made plans to visit us over the holidays.
    B) were planning to visit us over the holiday season.
    C) planned to visit us over the holidays.

19. Officer Johnson, one of the new officers, *were patrolling late last night*.

    A) were patrolling late last night.
    B) was patrolling late last night.
    C) would have been patrolling late last night.

**20.** Several suspects wanted *to speak at once to their attorneys*.

   **A)** to speak at once to their attorneys.

   **B)** to speak once to one of their attorneys.

   **C)** to speak to their attorneys immediately.

## Detail

In the following sentence pairs, identify the sentence that has the most detailed and useful information.

**21.**

   **A)** Officer Morales entered 341 Staples Street, the scene of an apparent physical altercation between a father, Joshua Randall, and his eight-year-old son. Officer Morales noticed evident bruising along the child's neck as well as apparent wheezing in his voice. Randall was taken into custody.

   **B)** At 12:42 p.m. on Thursday, March 4, Officer Morales entered 341 Staples Street in response to a call. He encountered Joshua Randall, a 34-year-old Caucasian male, and an eight-year-old Caucasian boy, identified as Randall's son. Officer Morales observed bruising on the child's neck as well as apparent wheezing in his voice. Randall was taken into custody without incident.

**22.**

   **A)** Officer Bridges was patrolling River City Park on Wednesday, October 23, when he noticed a car speeding through a stop sign at approximately 2:15 a.m. on Center Street. He pulled the car over for a routine traffic stop. He asked the driver, a 23-year-old male, to present his license and registration. At that time, Officer Bridges observed the smell of alcohol on the man.

   **B)** Officer Bridges is patrolling a city park around 2:15 a.m. when he notices a car speeding through a stop sign on the closest street. He pulled the car over for a routine traffic stop. When he asked the driver for his license and registration, he observed the smell of alcohol.

**23.**

   **A)** Officer Holmes arrived at the scene of an accident on Thursday, February 1, at 11:23 a.m. Kelly Porter, a motorist, reported that she did not see a cyclist riding in her blind spot. She hit him with her car as she made the right turn at 556 North Weatherview Lane.

   **B)** On Thursday, February 1, around 11:00 a.m., Kelly Porter, a motorist, reported that she did not see a cyclist riding in her blind spot. She hit him with her car as she made the right turn on North Weatherview Lane. Officer Holmes took the report.

**24.**

   **A)** Ronald Crawford, the victim of an attempted robbery, tells Officer Martinez that he was going to Giant Grocery Store to purchase groceries when a homeless man accosted him, asking him for money. Crawford says it was a little after 7:00 p.m. at 9876 Cherry Lane on Monday, July 18. Crawford is a 57-year-old African American male, and the homeless man was Caucasian and in his mid-twenties.

   **B)** Officer Martinez is interviewing Ronald Crawford, a 57-year-old African American male. Crawford, the victim of an attempted robbery, states that he was entering Giant Grocery Store on 9876 Cherry Lane shortly after 7:00 p.m. on Monday, July 18, to purchase groceries. At that time, a homeless man accosted him, asking him for money. The homeless man was Caucasian and in his mid-twenties.

**25.**

A) Officer Watson responded to a prowler call at 311 Center Street at the intersection of Sixteenth Street on Sunday, February 28, at 10:35 p.m. He is the first officer to arrive at the scene and waits for backup in his patrol car. A civilian approaches the officer. The civilian matches the description of the suspected prowler: a middle-aged male of medium build.

B) On Sunday evening, Officer Watson responded to a prowler call at Sixteenth and Center Streets. He is the first officer to arrive at the scene and waits for backup in his patrol car. A middle-aged male civilian approaches the officer. The civilian, who is of medium build, matches the description of the suspected prowler.

**26.**

A) Officer Bauser interviewed the witness to a fire, Jack Cho. Cho was on his way to work when he noticed a young man running away from a building. A moment later, he noticed the building was in flames. The young man was tall and very thin.

B) Officer Bauser interviewed the witness to a fire, Jack Cho, 39. On his way to work, Cho noticed a Hispanic male of slim build who appeared to be in his early twenties running away from a building. A moment later, Cho saw the building burst into flames.

**27.**

A) While Marta Lefkowitz, 34, was at work downtown, her house on the East Side was burglarized. The incident occurred on a hot day in June.

B) On Wednesday, June 30, Marta Lefkowitz, 34, reported that her house at 4673 East Meadow Lane was burglarized at approximately 3:00 p.m. Lefkowitz was at work at Downtown Manufacturers at the time.

**28.**

A) On Monday, September 20, at 8:40 a.m., Officer Gordon responded to an incident at 211 Big Sky Drive, the home of Dolores Pilconis, 62. She alleged that her black 2019 Ford Expedition was stolen. The last time Pilconis saw the vehicle was when she parked it across the street from her house at 2:00 a.m.

B) Officer Gordon responded to an incident at Mrs. Pilconis's home on September 20. She told him that her black 2019 Ford Expedition had been stolen, claiming that the last time she saw it was when she parked it across the street very late the night before.

## Word Usage

The following questions provide two word choices to complete the sentences below. Choose the word that makes the most sense based on the context of the sentence.

**29.** The tactical commander outlined the _____ of action for the SWAT team.

A) coarse

B) course

**30.** Increased penalties for criminal activity in River City did not appear to have an _____ on the occurrence of crime.

A) effect

B) affect

**31.** The nightly news reported that the police apprehended the _____ killer who had been tormenting River City residents.

A) cereal

B) serial

**32.** While on the job, it is our duty to uphold the _____ of good policing.

A) principles

B) principals

33. When Tom spoke at the town hall meeting, he intended his words to motivate people to fight for their rights, not to _____ a riot.
    A) incite
    B) insight

34. Mayor Brighton did not _____ whether Oscar's speech was protected by the First Amendment of the Constitution.
    A) know
    B) no

35. Jerry had not eaten in four days and had no money, so he decided to _____ some food to get by.
    A) steel
    B) steal

36. Deputy Wilson worked very hard to _____ her skills as an officer.
    A) home
    B) hone

37. Judge Singleton asked _____ the defendant was when he failed to appear.
    A) wear
    B) where

38. The officers made plans to _____ the witnesses on Monday afternoon.
    A) meet
    B) meat

39. After years of daily observing people in the worst situations of their lives, Austin's behavior became _____.
    A) callous
    B) callus

40. The severity of the crime _____ that the suspect would face a lengthy sentence.
    A) insured
    B) ensured

41. Officer Wilkinson did not want to interrupt the grieving wife while she was in _____, but he had many questions for her.
    A) morning
    B) mourning

42. The members of the jury had been waiting for hours; they were nearly out of _____.
    A) patience
    B) patients

43. The judge wanted to teach Justin a _____ and sentenced him to community service.
    A) lessen
    B) lesson

## Spelling

Read the following sentences and choose the correct spelling of the missing word.

44. John Smith told the court he did not recognize the authority of the _____ and was filing a lawsuit against it to reclaim money owed him as a right of birth.
    A) goverment
    B) govermant
    C) government

45. Officer uses of force are _____ and appropriate actions when suspects fail to comply and can escalate police contacts in a manner that jeopardizes safety.
    A) necessary
    B) nesisarry
    C) necissary

**46.** The jury foreman turned _____ the defendant when he read the verdict.
   A) tward
   B) toword
   C) toward

**47.** The District Attorney _____ dropped off the case files this morning.
   A) liason
   B) liaison
   C) laison

**48.** The legislature _____ the law when it was ruled unconstitutional.
   A) resinded
   B) recinded
   C) rescinded

**49.** Even the defendant was _____ when the jury returned a not-guilty verdict.
   A) surprised
   B) suprised
   C) supprised

**50.** Officer Jones had a _____ to speak loudly, which often upset people.
   A) tendancy
   B) tendency
   C) tendincy

**51.** The tension in the courtroom was _____ as the jury prepared to read the verdict.
   A) palpible
   B) palpable
   C) palpebal

**52.** The judge signed a _____ to compel the company to turn the phone records over to the police.
   A) subpena
   B) supeana
   C) subpoena

**53.** Judy was _____ of her son, who suddenly had a lot of money and rarely came home at night.
   A) suspicious
   B) suspisios
   C) suspiscious

**54.** At the scene of a car accident, Officer Garcia attempted to _____ the exchange of information between drivers because they were arguing with each other.
   A) fasilitate
   B) fascilitate
   C) facilitate

**55.** The suspect was _____ for four hours before he confessed.
   A) interrogated
   B) interogated
   C) interragated

**56.** Four _____ witnesses placed Harry at the scene of the crime.
   A) indapendant
   B) independent
   C) independant

**57.** As a victim of a _____ crime, Luis devoted his time to changing legislation regarding victims' rights.
   A) heinous
   B) hanous
   C) haneous

**58.** Gabriel was an _____ child who would not listen to his parents and continued to get into trouble.
   A) incorrigable
   B) incorrigible
   C) incorrigeable

44   Elissa Simon ■ MCOLES Study Guide

**59.** The child, who had asthma, was _____ and struggling to breathe when the officers arrived on the scene.

A) weezing

B) weazing

C) wheezing

**60.** We aren't allowed to take personal _____ calls at work unless it is an emergency.

A) telephone

B) teliphone

C) telaphone

# Reading

Read each paragraph or passage and choose the response that best answers the question. All questions are self-contained and use only information provided in the passage that precedes them.

With over twenty-two million staff members and students on college campuses across the nation, campus security has moved to the spotlight. Security staff have the opportunity to be proactive, educating the college community about campus life and being safe while in a home away from home.

Depending on the size and location of a given school, campus security staffing and scope might be either small-scale or <u>monolithically</u> entrenched in the campus community. Additionally, some campuses employ full-time police agencies, while others employ independent contractors or private security companies. However, because the nature and scope of each campus security department varies so widely, the level of communication with other security and law enforcement departments also varies, causing misunderstandings and errors in interdepartmental communication. Now is a crucial time, given the tragic events on school and college campuses and the sheer number of people continually on campuses, to begin creating universal standards so that all students and staff members have the same level of protection regardless of the school where they choose to study or work.

1. As used in the passage, what is the best definition of the word *monolithically*?

   A) stonelike
   B) impenetrable
   C) massive

2. The passage mentions that all of the following as employed as campus security EXCEPT

   A) security companies.
   B) private contractors.
   C) retired police officers.

3. According to the passage, what is an important problem that needs to be addressed?

   A) communication among agencies
   B) size of security agencies
   C) education of the campus community

4. Which of the following, if true, most WEAKENS the argument that the variation in size and scope of campus security departments is the cause of communication problems?

   A) Smaller operations have more money to spend on communications than large ones.
   B) Interoperability between campuses is based on size and scope.
   C) Each operation, regardless of size and scope, uses its own dedicated communication system.

5. Based on the tone of the passage, it can be inferred that the author believes which statement about campus security?

   A) Campus security operations are varied to the point of dysfunction.
   B) Size and scope do not necessarily matter if the operation functions properly
   C) Large campus security operations are safer than small ones.

(1)

Think cattle rustling is a thing of the past? Think again. As of March 2014, cattle rustling in the western United States is still "a thing." Ranchers and law enforcement are <u>diligently</u> working together to protect herds and keep them safe from a brand-new threat—meth addicts. People addicted to methamphetamine have turned in their climbing boots and copper wire–grabbing gloves to steal cows in order to finance their drug habits. Where's the *Outlaw Josey Wales* when you need him?

(2)

Levity aside, neither of the aforementioned issues is a laughing matter. Methamphetamine addiction is very serious, dangerous, and expensive to maintain. Issues surrounding the crime of cow theft is equally serious, dangerous, and expensive. Cows are valuable and can be sold at auction for around $1,000 a head. A local news station obtained video depicting thieves as they stole an entire pen of cows by coaxing them into the back of a big rig in the middle of the night. Another rancher had 100 cows stolen. At $1,000 a head, that's big money—and big jail time. Currently, cattle rustling carries penalties of up to ten years in prison. The problem for ranchers, while fortuitous for the thieves, is that it's fairly easy to avoid detection while selling stolen livestock at auction. Why? The cows often are not branded.

(3)

Why not simply brand the cows? Well, that depends on the rancher. Some ranchers seek support and endorsements from the Certified Humane Project (CHP), and organizations like it, for meat products. CHP grades livestock on a step level from 1 to 5, with 1 being the lowest and 5 being the highest. The higher the meat's rating, the more natural, healthy, and flavorful it is, allowing the farmer to command a premium price. As farmers desire to return to natural and humane ways of farming and cattle raising, while also increasing their earnings potential, fewer farmers are branding their cattle. If farmers treat their animals humanely and get their animals' habitat closer to what normally occurs in nature, the meat will have a higher rating when it finally makes it to the grocery stores.

(4)

One thing CHP has noted is that branding animals is not humane. As such, ranchers have a decision to make—protect the herd with brands or resist branding to achieve higher CHP step ratings. Either choice will likely cost them big bucks.

6. What is the main point of this passage?

   A) Cows are expensive.
   B) Cattle rustling is still a big problem for ranchers.
   C) Ranchers should brand their cows.

7. In paragraph 2, a rancher is said to have had 100 cows stolen. According to the article, what is the total monetary loss of the cows before processing?

   A) $1,000,000
   B) $10,000
   C) $100,000

8. According to the passage, what is a service that Certified Humane Project (CHP) provides?

   A) third-party evaluation of farms and animal habitat
   B) rate livestock and resultant meat products
   C) create benchmarks for organic humane food sources

9. The passage implies which is true about branding?

   A) Branding does not affect the animals.
   B) Branding is not a major issue for ranchers.
   C) Ranchers make more money if they don't brand.

10. The passage mentions each of the following EXCEPT

    A) cattle rustling as "big money" for meth addicts.
    B) copper as a source for addicts to fund their habits.
    C) services for addicts to overcome addiction.

11. Which of the words below most closely matches the meaning of the word *diligently* as used in the first paragraph?

    A) neglectful
    B) persistently
    C) unconcerned

**12.** Which of the following is a central dilemma for ranchers?

   A) It's easy to sell stolen cattle undetected because they are not branded, but branding the animals reduces their value.

   B) Ranchers often know the addicts who steal their cattle because they are community and family members, making it difficult to prosecute them.

   C) Branding cattle increases the value of the meat on the market, but it hurts the cows and is not humane.

---

Influenza (also called the flu) has historically been one of the most common, and deadliest, human infections. While many people who contract the virus will recover, many others will not. Over the past 150 years, tens of millions of people have died from the flu, and millions more have been left with lingering complications such as secondary infections.

Although it's a common disease, the flu is not actually highly infectious, meaning it's relatively difficult to contract. The flu can only be transmitted when individuals come into direct contact with bodily fluids of people infected with the flu or when they are exposed to expelled aerosol particles (which result from coughing and sneezing). Because the viruses can only travel short distances as aerosol particles and will die within a few hours on hard surfaces, the virus can be contained with fairly simple health measures like hand washing and face masks.

However, the spread of the flu can only be contained when people are aware such measures need to be taken. One of the reasons the flu has historically been so deadly is the amount of time between when people become infectious and when they develop symptoms. Viral shedding—the process by which the body releases viruses that have been successfully reproducing during the infection—takes place two days after infection, while symptoms do not usually develop until the third day of infection. Thus, infected individuals have at least twenty-four hours in which they may unknowingly infect others.

---

**13.** What is the main idea of the passage?

   A) The flu is a deadly disease that's difficult to control because people become infectious before they show symptoms.

   B) For the flu to be transmitted, individuals must come in contact with bodily fluids from infected individuals.

   C) The spread of the flu is easy to contain because the viruses do not live long either as aerosol particles or on hard surfaces.

**14.** Which of the following correctly describes the flu?

   A) The flu is easy to contract and always fatal.

   B) The flu is difficult to contract and always fatal.

   C) The flu is difficult to contract and sometimes fatal.

**15.** Why is the flu considered to NOT be highly infectious?

   A) Many people who get the flu will recover and have no lasting complications, so only a small number of people who become infected will die.

   B) The process of viral shedding takes two days, so infected individuals have enough time to implement simple health measures that stop the spread of the disease.

   C) The flu virus cannot travel far or live for long periods of time outside the human body, so its spread can easily be contained.

**16.** What is the meaning of the word *measures* in the last paragraph?

   A) a plan of action

   B) a standard unit

   C) an adequate amount

**17.** What can the reader conclude from the previous passage?

   **A)** Preemptively implementing health measures like hand washing and face masks could help stop the spread of the flu virus.

   **B)** Doctors are not sure how the flu virus is transmitted, so they are unsure how to stop it from spreading.

   **C)** The flu is dangerous because it is both deadly and highly infectious.

**18.** Which statement is NOT a detail from the passage?

   **A)** Tens of millions of people have been killed by the flu virus.

   **B)** There is typically a twenty-four-hour window during which individuals are infectious but not showing flu symptoms.

   **C)** Viral shedding is the process by which people recover from the flu.

---

The most important part of brewing coffee is getting the right water. Choose a water that you think has a nice, neutral flavor. Anything with too many minerals or contaminants will change the flavor of the coffee, and water with too few minerals won't do a good job of extracting the flavor from the coffee beans. Water should be heated to between 195 and 205 degrees Fahrenheit. Boiling water (212 degrees Fahrenheit) will burn the beans and give your coffee a scorched flavor.

While the water is heating, grind your beans. Remember, the fresher the grind, the fresher the flavor of the coffee. The number of beans is entirely dependent on your personal taste. Obviously, more beans will result in a more robust flavor, while fewer beans will give your coffee a more subtle taste. The texture of the grind should not be too fine (which can lead to bitter coffee) or too large (which can lead to weak coffee).

Once the beans are ground and the water has reached the perfect temperature, you're ready to brew. A French press (which we recommend), allows you to control brewing time and provide a thorough brew. Pour the grounds into the press, then pour the hot water over the grounds and let it steep. The brew shouldn't require more than five minutes, although those of you who like your coffee a bit harsher can leave it longer. Finally, use the plunger to remove the grounds and pour.

---

**19.** What is the author's intent in writing this passage?

   **A)** to describe how to make hot beverages

   **B)** to argue that grinding beans makes a better cup of coffee

   **C)** to explain how to brew a cup of coffee

**20.** Which of the following statements based on the passage should be considered an opinion?

   **A)** While the water is heating, grind your beans.

   **B)** A French press (which we recommend), allows you to control brewing time and provide a thorough brew.

   **C)** Anything with too many minerals or contaminants will change the flavor of the coffee, and water with too few minerals won't do a good job of extracting the flavor from the coffee beans.

**21.** According to the passage, which of the following lists the steps for brewing coffee in the correct sequence?

   **A)** Choose a water that doesn't have too many or two few minerals. Then, heat water to boiling and pour over coffee grounds.

   **B)** Grind the beans to the appropriate texture and pour into the French press. Then, heat water to boiling and pour over the ground beans. Finally, use the plunger to remove the grounds and pour.

   **C)** Choose the right type of water and heat it to the correct temperature. Next, grind the beans and put them in the French press. Then, pour the hot water over the grounds and let the coffee steep.

**22.** Which of the following best describes the structure of the text?

- **A)** chronological
- **B)** cause and effect
- **C)** problem and solution

**23.** Which of the following would be an appropriate title for this passage?

- **A)** How to Brew the Perfect Cup of Coffee
- **B)** Why Drinking Coffee Is the Best Way to Start the Day
- **C)** How to Use a French Press to Make Coffee

**24.** Which of the following conclusions is best supported by the passage?

- **A)** Coffee should never be brewed for longer than five minutes.
- **B)** It's better to use too many coffee beans when making coffee than too few.
- **C)** The best way to brew coffee is often determined by personal preferences.

---

Medical professionals not only have to handle physical medical emergencies; they also have to be prepared to manage behavioral emergencies. Behavioral emergencies occur when a person's behavior—an observable response to the environment—is unreasonable to the point that it disrupts normal, everyday activities. Extreme cases of a behavioral emergency may result when someone's behavior is creating a danger to themselves or others. Chronic cases of extreme behavioral emergencies may eventually be classified as a mental disorder. Psychological and behavioral effects can result from any number of illnesses; they can also be the result of a chemical imbalance, genetic disorder, or psychological disturbance. People suffering from mental disorders are at risk for increased incidents of behavioral emergencies because their behavioral patterns are typically impaired or disrupted. Consequently, medical professionals must be trained in crisis management to deal with behavioral emergencies that may increase the possibility of self-harm or interpersonal conflict. While medical practitioners must be trained for emergency situations that demand physical restraint, extreme cases of behavioral emergency may be directed to police for appropriate support.

---

**25.** Which of the following statements can the reader infer from the passage?

- **A)** People who are mentally ill are harder to deal with than physically ill patients.
- **B)** Most people who are psychologically disturbed try to harm themselves or others.
- **C)** In a behavioral emergency, police officers may have to put handcuffs on a mentally ill person.

**26.** What is the author's primary purpose in writing this paragraph?

- **A)** to inform readers about managing patients in behavioral emergencies
- **B)** to persuade family members to call 911 to prevent suicides
- **C)** to advise readers about ways to treat someone who is mentally ill

**27.** Which of the following statements can be considered a statement of FACT according to the content offered in the paragraph above?

- **A)** It is unlawful for a medical professional to attempt to treat a violent, mentally ill patient without calling for police assistance.
- **B)** When a person's actions pose a threat to him- or herself—or to others—professionals consider this an extreme form of behavioral emergency.
- **C)** People suffering from mental illness almost always cause behavioral emergencies because they cannot stop themselves from picking fights with others.

**28.** According to the passage, what is true of genetic disorders?

- **A)** They are one cause of mental illness.
- **B)** They do not cause mental illness.
- **C)** They almost always cause mental illness.

29. According to the passage, when should a medical professional call for police support in dealing with a behavioral emergency?

    A) in every case
    B) very rarely
    C) when the medical professional needs help with physically restraining someone

> While smoking remains a public health concern for politicians and medical practitioners, a new epidemic has entered the media's sights: drug overdoses. Over 70,000 people in the United States died from drug overdoses in 2017; 68 percent of those involved opioids. This epidemic began in the late 1990s with the overprescription of legal drugs for pain management—pharmaceutical companies downplayed their addictive qualities—and their subsequent misuse.
>
> In particular, one extremely powerful opioid has raised the concerns of law enforcement officials and medical professionals: fentanyl. Fentanyl and its close cousins, oxycodone (commonly known by its brand name, Oxycontin, or just "oxy") and methadone, have made the leap from prescription drugs to street fare. Now add drugs such as heroin into the mix. Fentanyl, which is fifty times more potent than heroin, is mixed with heroin for sale on the street, leading to more overdoses from street drugs than ever before.
>
> The impact of the opioid epidemic has been so devastating that the life expectancy for men—who disproportionately die from overdoses—has decreased in recent years. In particular, the number of deaths between the ages of twenty-five and fifty-four has increased, largely because this is the prime age range for risky drug use. White people account for the majority of opioid-related deaths, and the epidemic has hit hard in rural communities and among veterans. Government officials are focusing on drug prevention and rehabilitation programs, and the epidemic has been declared a public health emergency.

30. Which sentence best summarizes the passage's main idea?

    A) In the United States there is an epidemic of opioid drug overdoses.
    B) The majority of users who die from opioid drug overdoses are white people.
    C) Politicians and medical practitioners still consider smoking a public health concern.

31. What is the meaning of the word *concern* in the first sentence?

    A) distressed state
    B) fretfulness
    C) worrisome matter

32. What is the author's primary purpose in writing this essay?

    A) to reassure readers that public health officials have the opioid crisis well in hand
    B) to inform readers that opioid drug overdoses are a serious problem in the United States
    C) to persuade opioid drug users to enter treatment as soon as possible

33. Which of the following is NOT listed as a detail in the passage?

    A) Drug companies that manufacture opioids are taking responsibility for the opioid epidemic.
    B) Of the 70,000 drug overdoses in 2017, 68 percent were related to opioids.
    C) Fentanyl and Oxycontin, once available only by prescription, are now sold illegally on the street.

34. Readers can infer from reading this passage that public health officials have not yet _____.

    A) learned what causes drug overdoses in the United States
    B) gotten the opioid drug overdose epidemic under control
    C) studied pharmaceutical drug companies' role in selling addictive pain killers

Hand washing is one of our simplest and most powerful weapons against infection. The idea behind hand washing is deceptively simple. Many illnesses are spread when people touch infected surfaces, such as door handles or other people's hands, and then touch their own eyes, mouths, or noses. So, if pathogens can be removed from the hands before they spread, infections can be prevented. When done correctly, hand washing can prevent the spread of many dangerous bacteria and viruses, including those that cause the flu, the common cold, diarrhea, and many acute respiratory illnesses.

The most basic method of hand washing involves only soap and water. Just twenty seconds of scrubbing with soap and a complete rinsing with water is enough to kill and/or wash away many pathogens. The process doesn't even require warm water—studies have shown that cold water is just as effective at reducing the number of microbes on the hands. Antibacterial soaps are also available, although several studies have shown that simple soap and cold water are just as effective.

In recent years, hand sanitizers have become popular as an alternative to hand washing. These gels, liquids, and foams contain a high concentration of alcohol (usually at least 60 percent) that kills most bacteria and fungi; they can also be effective against some, but not all, viruses. There is a downside to hand sanitizer, however. Because the sanitizer isn't rinsed from hands, it only kills pathogens and does nothing to remove organic matter. So, hands "cleaned" with hand sanitizer may still harbor pathogens. Thus, while hand sanitizer can be helpful in situations where soap and clean water isn't available, a simple hand washing is still the best option.

**35.** Which of the following is not a fact stated in the passage?

   **A)** Many infections occur because people get pathogens on their hands and then touch their own eyes, mouths, or noses.

   **B)** Antibacterial soaps and warm water are the best way to remove pathogens from hands.

   **C)** Most hand sanitizers have a concentration of at least 60 percent alcohol.

**36.** What is the best summary of this passage?

   **A)** Many diseases are spread by pathogens that can live on the hands. Hand washing is the best way to remove these pathogens and prevent disease.

   **B)** Simple hand washing can prevent the spread of many common illnesses, including the flu, the common cold, diarrhea, and many acute respiratory illnesses. Hand sanitizer can also kill the pathogens that cause these diseases.

   **C)** Simple hand washing with soap and cold water is an effective way to reduce the spread of disease. Antibacterial soaps and hand sanitizers may also be used but are not significantly more effective.

**37.** What is the meaning of the word *harbor* in the last paragraph?

   **A)** to disguise

   **B)** to hide

   **C)** to give a home

**38.** Knowing that the temperature of the water does not affect the efficacy of hand washing, one can conclude that water plays an important role in hand washing because it

   **A)** has antibacterial properties.

   **B)** physically removes pathogens from hands.

   **C)** cools hands to make them inhospitable to dangerous bacteria.

**39.** What is the author's primary purpose in writing this essay?

   **A)** to persuade readers of the importance and effectiveness of hand washing with soap and cold water

   **B)** to dissuade readers from using hand sanitizer

   **C)** to explain how many common diseases are spread through daily interaction

**40.** What can the reader conclude from the passage?

   **A)** Hand washing would do little to limit infections that spread through particles in the air.

   **B)** Hand washing is not necessary for people who do not touch their eyes, mouths, or noses with their hands.

   **C)** Hand sanitizer serves no purpose and should not be used as an alternative to hand washing.

---

**(1)**

When people think critically, they examine, evaluate, and synthesize information they have gathered in order to arrive at a logical conclusion. Critical thinking can be accomplished at a simple or more probing level, depending on whether a cursory or more thoughtful conclusion is desired. At its most basic level, critical thinking is an activity necessary for people to function properly in society. Every day, without thought, most people engage in simple critical thinking exercises as they interact with one another. They observe, analyze, and assess clues and information around them in order to understand others' behavior and to make decisions about how to respond appropriately. When used purposefully, critical thinking can help one gain a much greater understanding of the gathered information. However, many people do not wish to move beyond this basic, instinctual level when deep critical thinking is not <u>imperative</u>. They do not wish to gain deeper understanding of a person or issue even though gaining such understanding may be as simple as asking, "Why?"

**(2)**

Intensive critical thinking is employed most often in academic settings. Teachers challenge students to apply a higher order of thinking skills to avoid oversimplification, to be objective, and to always ask the next question such as "Why?" "What?" or "What if?" to make reasoned judgments. Critical thinking in academia generally requires a supposition, facts and information, and the ability to infer a logical conclusion from one or more assertions. In academia, critical thinking can either be relegated to mere theoretical dialogue or be applied to an actual problem in order to generate improved conditions.

**(3)**

Since the 1970s, critical thinking has also been used in police work. It is vital, purposeful, and systematic. Police must analyze crimes and criminal activity, establish facts, and determine what information remains unknown. Police investigators analyze patterns and evidence to determine how and why criminal activity was committed and who committed the crime. They ask the questions "What's missing?" "What are the benefits of the crime?" "Who benefited?" "Was the crime planned or opportunistic?" Each question probes deeper into the issue and helps investigators uncover clues to reconstruct other people's reasoning. Critical thinking in police work questions the known facts of a case in such a way that investigators are able to understand criminal actions, and those who commit them, more accurately. Such thinking can help investigators understand a perpetrator's state of mind, determine what the perpetrator was thinking, how he or she was thinking, as well as establish the investigator's opinion of what, how, and why a particular event occurred.

**(4)**

Recently, critical thinking has become even more vital to law enforcement because criminals continue to become more <u>savvy</u>. As technology has evolved, so has crime sophistication. Criminals have to work smarter to avoid being apprehended, thus detectives work smarter by studying, evaluating, and assessing evidence to successfully investigate and prosecute criminals.

---

**41.** The tone of the author can be best described as what?

   **A)** objective

   **B)** argumentative

   **C)** passionate

**42.** As used in paragraph 1, what is the best synonym for *imperative*?

   **A)** absolutely necessary

   **B)** very important

   **C)** of personal interest

**43.** According to the passage, it can be inferred that the author believes which of the following?

   I.  Critical thinking is used in many ways.
   II. Critical thinking is only important in academia.
   III. Critical thinking is vital in police work.

   A) III only
   B) I and III only
   C) II and III only

**45.** As used in paragraph 4, what is the best definition of *savvy*?

   A) cool
   B) shrewd
   C) inexperienced

**44.** Which of the following, if true, WEAKENS the main point of paragraph 3?

   A) People do not use critical thinking in everyday life.
   B) Law enforcement began using critical thinking methods in the 1990s.
   C) Critical thinking has reduced successful investigations and prosecutions of crimes.

**46.** What is the best title for this passage?

   A) The Definition of Critical Thinking
   B) Critical Thinking and Law Enforcement
   C) The Many Applications of Critical Thinking

---

River City Police Department policy mandates that officers remain in good physical condition while employed with the department. Most officers would gladly comply, but commute times, long work hours, and mandatory overtime account for about fifteen hours of each officer's day. Officers recently asked River City about developing a wellness program for staff members, sworn staff in particular, including the ability to exercise in one of the many gyms located at various River City Police Department's satellite facilities. The resulting memo from the River City chief of police was disseminated to all staff.

---

Dear Staff,

It gives me great pleasure to work at an agency that is full of hardworking, motivated individuals, sworn and civilians alike, who seek new ways to continue improving themselves in both professional and personal life.

As you are aware, law enforcement is a physical job that requires the men and women who do the job to maintain a high level of physical fitness. I'm confident all of you would like to maintain that high level of physical fitness. I know this is difficult for many who have family obligations and long commutes from your respective homes in the outlying areas, and for those who work copious overtime shifts. These factors have undoubtedly created barriers for you to reach your personal goals and the required baseline goals of this department.

It was recently brought to my attention that a number of you requested permission to exercise at your duty station during your workday, on your meal break, in one of the various gyms we maintain on facility sites, in order to make exercising easier to fit into your daily routine. I understand your various dilemmas, but for reasons of liability, workers' compensation issues, as well as the logistical issues involved in managing meal breaks so an entire duty station is not working out at the same time, I must deny that request. I will, however, work with you in other ways to help you meet your fitness goals.

As of next week, the following policies will take effect under the River City Police Employee Wellness Pledge program:

- We will update our meal program for staff members assigned to duty stations where leaving base during shifts is disallowed. We will no longer provide hamburgers, soda, french fries, bacon, or chips. For those of you who work the night shift and eat breakfast, eggs and hash brown potatoes will still be available. If you would like to purchase a soda or snack during your twelve-hour shift, you may do so at the remaining vending machines on-site.

- You may not exercise at any gym during duty hours, even if you are on break. You are welcome to work out before or after your assigned shift at any of our gyms.
- We will begin a physical fitness club that will meet once a month at one of our facilities for organized workouts. This club is open to the first 30 people who sign up. I, as well as the <u>warriors</u> who already work out with me, would love for you to join us at our morning gym sessions.

Thank you for your diligence to do the job well and to make River City the best police department in the state. I look forward to helping you meet your fitness goals and to your feedback on this exciting new program.

Keep up the good work!

Sincerely,

Chief Jeff Hyde

**47.** What is the main point of the chief's letter?

A) Physical fitness is important for police work.

B) The chief is willing to help officers and staff stay fit.

C) It is primarily the responsibility of the employee to manage time for workouts.

**48.** What is the best meaning of the word *warriors* as used in the passage?

A) a person experienced in warfare

B) a person who shows great vigor

C) a person skilled in using weapons

**49.** What is the overall tone of the chief's letter?

A) cordial

B) angry

C) passionate

**50.** According to the passage, how many hours in a given day does the average River City officer have left to eat, sleep, run errands, and work out after he or she has completed duty hours?

A) fifteen

B) seventeen

C) nine

(1)

Since the police usually do not have the opportunity to watch a crime as it happens, they must rely on evidence, statements from witnesses and involved parties, and deduction skills to draw conclusions about what actually occurred. Although reliance on information from others is essential, the information officers receive is often inaccurate either because the individual was mistaken in his or her perception, was biased, or was purposefully deceptive. Police must skillfully sift through all the information they receive and decide which is accurate and which is not. The officer's decision is generally based on his or her assessment of the information's source and whether it is credible or reliable. There are three main reasons information is unreliable.

(2)

The most frequent type of unreliable information is mistaken perception. Mistaken perception happens when otherwise honest and reliable people give information they believe to be true but is not. Mistaken perception can happen for a number of reasons. For example, during a stressful situation the brain releases adrenaline into the body, causing physiological changes. During periods of extreme stress, blood rushes away from nonessential organs and systems toward the heart. As this happens, people often experience various sensory disturbances, like time anomalies. Often witnesses and involved parties will report that a greater or lesser amount of time passed than actually did. A time <u>anomaly</u> affects an individual's sense of time, which appears to be moving at lightning speed or in slow motion. Sight and sound may also be affected. Witnesses and involved parties experiencing auditory occlusion often describe a temporary loss or lessening of hearing; sounds are muted or unheard. People also experience the feeling of tunnel vision, wherein peripheral vision is diminished and they can only see what is directly in front of them. People who undergo these physiological changes, even when mild, may have a distorted perception of the incident even though they are telling the truth based on their recollection. Police officers must pay attention to behavior cues that signal an individual may have altered perception due to physiological disturbances.

(3)

Another issue with involved party reliability is individual bias. While some people have biases they are aware of, sometimes people have biases they are unaware of for a number of reasons. The bias may stem from accepting another source of information as true without question. In other words, the individual was uncritical of the information received and then passed along to police. People also may have a bias due to a vested interest in a particular view or outcome, and their perception is altered by that interest. Police officers must be diligent in identifying any possible biases during the interview process when establishing witness accuracy and reliability.

(4)

Lastly, there are times when people are simply dishonest. The reason for their dishonesty may have nothing to do with the situation at hand. The motivation for the dishonesty may or may not be relevant to the incident, but it is crucial when determining the reliability of the statement itself. If a person is willing to be dishonest to the police, for whatever reason, his or her credibility must also be called into question. Police officers must pay attention to accounts of an incident by witnesses and involved parties for inconsistencies and blatant misinformation.

(5)

There are many reasons why accounts of an incident by witnesses and involved parties might be unreliable. It is the officer's duty to use critical thinking, deduction, and logical reasoning to determine what is or is not reliable and why. Police officers have a variety of tools at their disposal in order to determine the accuracy of witness or involved party statements. Corroboration, witness expertise, police officer observations, evidence located at the scene, and the like, can help an officer analyze the information to determine the probable reliability of a statement.

**51.** What is the main point of this article?

A) Witnesses are dishonest.

B) Witnesses can be unreliable.

C) Stress can alter witnesses' perception.

**52.** According to this article, what is the main reason for problems with witness reliability?

A) dishonesty

B) mistaken perception

C) both A and B

**53.** According to the passage, which of the following is true?

A) People only lie for reasons related to the situation.

B) Some people are unaware of bias they hold.

C) During high-stress situations, blood rushes away from the heart.

**54.** According to the passage, what is auditory occlusion?

A) total loss of hearing

B) tunnel vision

C) a temporary loss or lessening of hearing

**55.** What is the best synonym for the word *anomaly* as it is used in paragraph 2 of the passage?

A) commonality

B) ambivalence

C) abnormality

**56.** What word below is the best meaning of the word *blatant* as it is used in paragraph 4 of the passage?

A) obvious

B) flagrant

C) subtle

**57.** The passage implies which of the following?

   **A)** Because witnesses are often unreliable, officers must be diligent in their investigation.

   **B)** Witnesses are never reliable; officers must use other evidence to prove crimes.

   **C)** The most frequent type of unreliable information is individual bias.

---

We've been told for years that the recipe for weight loss is fewer calories in than calories out. In other words, eat less and exercise more, and your body will take care of the rest. As many of those who've tried to diet can attest, this edict doesn't always produce results. If you're one of those folks, you might have felt that you just weren't doing it right—that the failure was all your fault.

However, several new studies released this year have suggested that it might not be your fault at all. For example, a study of people who'd lost a high percentage of their body weight (>17%) in a short period of time found that they could not physically maintain their new weight. Scientists measured their resting metabolic rate and found that they'd need to consume only a few hundred calories a day to meet their metabolic needs. Basically, their bodies were in starvation mode and seemed to desperately hang on to each and every calorie. Eating even a single healthy, well-balanced meal a day would cause these subjects to start packing back on the pounds.

Other studies have shown that factors like intestinal bacteria, distribution of body fat, and hormone levels can affect the manner in which our bodies process calories. There's also the fact that it's actually quite difficult to measure the number of calories consumed during a particular meal and the number used while exercising.

---

**58.** Which of the following would be the best summary statement to conclude the passage?

   **A)** It turns out that conventional dieting wisdom doesn't capture the whole picture of how our bodies function.

   **B)** Still, counting calories and tracking exercise is a good idea if you want to lose weight.

   **C)** In conclusion, it's important to lose weight responsibly: losing too much weight at once can negatively impact the body.

**59.** Which of the following type of arguments is used in the passage?

   **A)** emotional argument

   **B)** appeal to authority

   **C)** specific evidence

**60.** Which of the following would weaken the author's argument?

   **A)** a new diet pill from a pharmaceutical company that promises to help patients lose weight by changing intestinal bacteria

   **B)** the personal experience of a man who was able to lose a significant amount of weight by taking in fewer calories than he used

   **C)** a study showing that people often misreport their food intake when part of a scientific study on weight loss

# ANSWER KEY

## Writing

1. **B) is correct.** This sentence has a grammar error. The contraction *it's* should be changed to the possessive pronoun *its*, which agrees with the antecedent *volcano*.

2. **B) is correct.** This sentence has a grammar error. The word *their* should be changed to the singular possessive pronoun *its* to agree with *grass*, a noncountable singular pronoun.

3. **A) is correct.** This sentence has no errors. *Grandchildren* and *cousins* are plural and so take the plural pronoun *their*.

4. **B) is correct.** The sentence contains an error—a double negative. The negative modifier "The employer decided that he could *not*…afford…") creates a double negative with the negative modifier "*no other benefits.*"

5. **B) is correct.** This sentence contains an error—an unnecessary apostrophe. Replace *it's* with the singular possessive pronoun *its* to match the singular antecedent *Puerto Rico*.

6. **A) is correct.** There are no errors in this sentence. The sentence states a general fact (how seat belts work), and so it should be written in present (or past) tense. The verb must be plural, since its subject, *Engineers*, is plural.

7. **A) is correct.** This sentence is grammatically correct. *Has* is a singular verb, referring to a singular noun (*Neptune*); *seasons* is the direct object of the verb *has*. *Seasons* must be plural to take the plural verb *last*.

8. **B) is correct.** This sentence is incorrect. *Animals* is plural, so it does not agree with the singular pronoun *it*.

9. **A) is correct.** The sentence has no error. The plural verb *are* agrees with its plural subject *paintings*.

10. **B) is correct.** This sentence is grammatically incorrect. The verb *offer* is conjugated incorrectly. The subject "Iris and B. Gerald Cantor Roof Garden" is singular, so the verb should be singular: *offers*.

11. **A) is correct.** Answers B and C are vague. It is not clear whose supervisor wishes to speak with which employee. Also, C is wordy.

12. **A) is correct.** Answers B and C contain a misplaced modifier: *in bags*. It is unclear whether the lunches or the deputies were in bags. Answer C is also wordy.

13. **C) is correct.** Answers A and B contain a misplaced modifier. It is not clear if officers who train are caught off guard infrequently, or if officers who train infrequently are caught off guard. Also, answer B incorrectly uses the relative pronoun *that* instead of *who*, which is needed because the antecedent *Officers* refers to people.

14. **A) is correct.** Answer B contains the vague pronoun *it*. It is not clear what Fran kept hidden. Answer A specifies what Fran kept hidden: *her fear*. Choice C is wordy and vague, incorrectly using the pronoun *that*.

15. **A) is correct.** Answer A is the clearest answer, with no dangling modifiers.

16. **C) is correct.** Answer C is the most clear and concise choice. Choices A and B are wordy.

17. **B) is correct.** Choice A contains a vague reference. It is unclear to whom the pronoun *they* refers. Choice C is wordy with unnecessary use of the passive voice.

18. **C) is correct.** Answer C is the most concise choice. Choices A and B are wordy.

19. **B) is correct.** Answer B correctly matches the verb with the singular subject *Officer Johnson*. Answer A uses an incorrect verb. Answer C changes the meaning of the sentence.

20. **C) is correct.** Answer C is the clearest statement. Answer A makes it sound like all the suspects want to speak at the same time. Answer B makes it sound like there is only one attorney.

21. **B) is correct.** Choice B provides more details: the date and time of the incident and Joshua Randall's age.

22. **A) is correct.** Choice A provides more details about the time and place of the incident and a description of the driver.

23. **A) is correct.** Sentence A contains slightly more information (the exact time and address of the accident) and is more clearly written.

24. **B) is correct.** Both choices contain plenty of details, but only choice B lays out the events in order, communicating them clearly.

25. **A) is correct.** Choice A contains more details about time and location, and more clearly describes the alleged prowler.

26. **B) is correct.** Choice B describes the suspect more clearly and in more detail; it also notes the witness's age.

27. **B) is correct.** Choice B contains more information about the time and location of the alleged burglary. Choice A notes that the day was "hot," but this is not as useful as the exact date. Choice A also notes that Ms. Lefkowitz was "downtown," but choice B contains her actual place of employment, which might be more useful.

28. **A) is correct.** Choice A contains more details and is written more clearly.

29. **B) is correct.** In this context, *course* means "manner of procedure." *Coarse* is a homonym and means "harsh" or "grating."

30. **A) is correct.** *Effect* as used in this context is a noun. Generally (though there are exceptions), the word *affect* is a verb, and *effect* is a noun. To *affect* is to "act upon something to cause change," as in "The snow *affected* his ability to drive." An *effect* is a result, as in "The snow had a negative *effect* on the undercarriage of his car." In the question, the "increased penalties" had no *effect* on crime.

31. **B) is correct.** In this context, *serial* means "producing a series of similar actions," such as killing. *Cereal* is an edible grain.

32. **A) is correct.** The word *principles*, which means "codes, morals, doctrines," is a noun. *Principal* is a noun when it refers to a person, like the head of a school; otherwise it is an adjective.

33. **A) is correct.** *Incite* means to urge or encourage. *Insight* is "the ability to see an underlying truth."

34. **A) is correct.** To *know* means to have knowledge of something. *No* is used to show dissent or denial.

35. **B) is correct.** *Steal* means to take another's property without permission. *Steel* is a type of metal.

36. **B) is correct.** To *hone* is to sharpen. A *home* is a dwelling where people reside.

37. **B) is correct.** *Where* is used to refer to place. *Wear* means "to put on," usually in reference to clothing.

38. **A) is correct.** To *meet* is to see or spend time with someone. *Meat* is the flesh of an animal.

39. **A) is correct.** *Callous* means "insensitive." A *callus* is a hardened area of skin.

40. **B) is correct.** To *ensure* is to make sure of something. *Insure* usually refers to insurance.

41. **B) is correct.** *Mourning* refers to grieving or sadness. *Morning* is the start of the day.

42. **A) is correct.** *Patience* is the state of tolerating annoyances. *Patients* are people receiving medical care.

43. **B) is correct.** A *lesson* is teaching or a tIme of learning. To *lessen* is to mitigate or make something less or weaker.

44. **C) is correct,** *government*.

45. **A) is correct,** *necessary*.

46. **C) is correct,** *toward*.

47. **B) is correct,** *liaison*.

48. **C) is correct** *rescinded*.

49. **A) is correct** *surprised*.

50. **B) is correct,** *tendency*.

51. **B) is correct,** *palpable*.

52. **C) is correct,** *subpoena*.

53. **A) is correct,** *suspicious*.

54. **C) is correct,** *facilitate*.

55. **A) is correct,** *interrogated*.

56. **B) is correct,** *independent*.

57. **A) is correct,** *heinous*.

58. **B) is correct,** *incorrigible*.

59. **C) is correct,** *wheezing*.

60. **A) is correct,** *telephone*.

# Reading

1. **C) is correct.** *Monolithically* means *massively*. It can also mean *stonelike*, but in this context choice C is the better answer; the passage suggests the agency is massive in contrast to "small-scale."

2. **C) is correct.** The passage mentions security companies, law enforcement, and contractors as agencies employed as campus security. It does not mention retired police officers specifically.

3. **A) is correct.** According to the passage, "because the nature and scope of each campus security department varies so widely, the level of communication with other security and law enforcement departments also varies, causing misunderstandings and errors in interdepartmental communication."

4. **C) is correct.** The passage mentions that the varying size and scope of different agencies make it difficult for them to communicate with one another. If each agency used its own dedicated communication system, then these communication systems would be the reason for interagency communication problems rather than the variation in size and scope of the agencies.

5. **B) is correct.** The author does not make a judgment about any specific type of security agency. Therefore, it can be inferred from the passage that the author believes that size and scope of a security department or operation do not matter as long as the operation functions properly.

6. **B) is correct.** The overall point of the passage is that ranchers still suffer from cattle rustling. The passage addresses the issues of cost, meat certifications, and branding, but these are not the main ideas of the passage.

7. **C) is correct.** The rancher lost $100,000. Multiply 100 cows by $1,000 per cow: 100 × 1000 = $100,000.

8. **B) is correct.** According to the passage, "CHP grades livestock on a step level from 1 to 5, with 1 being the lowest and 5 being the highest. The higher the meat's rating, the more natural, healthy, and flavorful it is, allowing the farmer to command a premium price."

9. **C) is correct.** The passage says that a higher rating from the CHP results in a higher price for meat; the CHP recommends against branding, making C the best choice.

10. **C) is correct.** The passage never discusses services to help addicts overcome addiction.

11. **B) is correct.** *Diligently* means persistently.

12. **A) is correct.** In paragraph 2, the passage states that the "problem for ranchers...is that it's fairly easy to avoid detection while selling stolen livestock at auction. Why? The cows often are not branded." However, paragraph 3 discusses how higher ratings from the Certified Humane Project (CHP) mean meat fetches higher prices at market, and in paragraph 4 the author writes, "ranchers have a decision to make—protect the herd with brands or resist branding to achieve higher CHP step ratings."

13. **A) is correct.** This choice addresses all of the main ideas of the passage: the flu is potentially deadly, highly infectious, and difficult to contain due to viral shedding.

14. **C) is correct.** According to the passage, "the flu is...relatively difficult to contract," and "while many people who contract the virus will recover, many others will not."

15. **C) is correct.** The second paragraph states that the flu is "relatively difficult to contract" because it "can only be transmitted when individuals come into direct contact with bodily fluids of people infected with the flu or when they are exposed to expelled aerosol particles."

16. **A) is correct.** The author uses the term *measures* to describe the steps that people

take to prevent the spreading of the influenza virus.

17. **A) is correct.** The second paragraph of the passage states that "the virus can be contained with fairly simple health measures like hand washing and face masks."

18. **C) is correct.** The final paragraph of the passage states that viral shedding is "the process by which the body releases viruses that have been successfully reproducing during the infection."

19. **C) is correct.** This passage is a step-by-step explanation of how to brew a cup of coffee.

20. **B) is correct.** The writer uses the first person, showing his or her opinion, to recommend a French press as the best way to brew coffee.

21. **C) is correct.** This choice lists the steps for brewing coffee in the same order as the passage.

22. **A) is correct.** The author describes the steps for making coffee in chronological order.

23. **A) is correct.** The passage as a whole describes from start to finish how to make a cup of coffee the drinker will enjoy.

24. **C) is correct.** The passage mentions several times that decisions about things like water minerals, ground size, and steep time will depend on the preference of the coffee drinker.

25. **C) is correct.** In the last sentence, the author states, "While medical practitioners must be trained for emergency situations that demand physical restraint, extreme cases of behavioral emergency may be directed to police for appropriate support." The reader can infer from this information that "physical restraint" means handcuffing or otherwise restraining a mentally ill patient who is violent.

26. **A) is correct.** The primary purpose of the essay is to inform; its focus is on managing behavioral emergencies. It is not persuasive or cautionary. It does not deal with treating mentally ill patients.

27. **B) is correct.** In the third sentence, the author writes, "Extreme cases of a behavioral emergency may result when someone's behavior is creating a danger to themselves or others."

28. **A) is correct.** The author writes, "Psychological and behavioral effects can result from any number of illnesses; they can also be the result of a chemical imbalance, genetic disorder, or psychological disturbance." There are no sentences supporting the other claims.

29. **C) is correct.** In the last sentence, the author writes, "While medical practitioners must be trained for emergency situations that demand physical restraint, extreme cases of behavioral emergency may be directed to police for appropriate support."

30. **A) is correct.** The passage is mainly about the epidemic of opioid drug overdoses. The other sentences give details from the passage.

31. **C) is correct.** In the first sentence, the author writes, "While smoking remains a public health concern for politicians and medical practitioners, a new epidemic has entered the media's sights: drug overdoses." Readers can use context to infer that by "a public health concern," the author means "a public health matter that worries people."

32. **B) is correct.** The passage is primarily informative, but there is an underlying cautionary message to take the drug overdose epidemic seriously: it kills many thousands of people each year. The passage is not reassuring or persuasive, and it does not tell a story about a specific drug dealer, though it mentions that on the street, fentanyl mixed with heroin is sold.

33. **A) is correct.** The passage does not contain this detail. The passage refers to drug companies in this sentence only: "This epidemic began in the late 1990s with the overprescription of legal drugs for pain

management—pharmaceutical companies downplayed their addictive qualities—and their subsequent misuse."

34. **B) is correct.** In the last paragraph, the author writes, "Government officials are focusing on drug prevention and rehabilitation programs, and the epidemic has been declared a public health emergency." Readers can infer that government officials are working hard on the problem but have not yet solved it.

35. **B) is correct.** In the second paragraph, the author writes, "The [hand washing] process doesn't even require warm water—studies have shown that cold water is just as effective at reducing the number of microbes on the hands. Antibacterial soaps are also available, although several studies have shown that simple soap and cold water are just as effective."

36. **C) is correct.** Together, these sentences provide an adequate summary of the passage overall.

37. **C) is correct.** The author writes that "hands 'cleaned' with hand sanitizer may still harbor pathogens" because sanitizer "does nothing to remove organic matter" from the hands. The bacteria are not completely washed off, and therefore some are able to continue living on the surface of the hands.

38. **B) is correct.** The author writes that because hand sanitizer "isn't rinsed from hands [as is water], it only kills pathogens and does nothing to remove organic matter."

39. **A) is correct.** Each paragraph examines hand washing from a different angle.

40. **A) is correct.** In the first paragraph, the author writes, "Many illnesses are spread when people touch infected surfaces, such as door handles or other people's hands, and then touch their own eyes, mouths, or noses." The reader can infer from this sentence that hand washing prevents the spread of surface-borne illnesses.

41. **A) is correct.** The passage is written with an impersonal objective tone, much like an article or news report, rather than to persuade or debate.

42. **A) is correct.** In this context, *imperative* means absolutely necessary. The passage asserts that "many people do not wish to move beyond this basic, instinctual level" of thought to critical thinking unless they must.

43. **B) is correct.** Only I and III are true. Option II, which states critical thinking is *only* important in academia, contradicts the first sentence of paragraph 3: "Since the 1970s, critical thinking has also been used in police work." In fact, the point of the passage is that critical thinking is vital to police work (choice III).

44. **B) is correct.** The definition of *savvy* is shrewd. This paragraph states that policing requires critical thinking to outsmart criminals.

45. **C) is correct.** If fewer crimes were successfully investigated and prosecuted since police began using critical thinking in investigations, then it would appear critical thinking is not helpful in police work. The purpose of paragraph 3 is to illustrate the many ways critical thinking has been used and can help in law enforcement.

46. **B) is correct.** The best title for this passage is "Critical Thinking and Law Enforcement." Although the passage defines critical thinking and illustrates its various applications, the bulk of the passage talks about the application of critical thinking to law enforcement. Thus answer B is the best choice.

47. **C) is correct.** The chief's letter identifies personal reasons why many people cannot schedule exercise into their daily routines. It also mentions the "warriors" who do work out in the morning, and the liability issues around allowing staff to exercise during shifts. Thus, C is the best answer; the chief will help, but he puts the responsibility on the employee to manage his or her time.

48. **B) is correct.** As used in the passage, the chief implies the "warriors" who work out every morning with him show motivation, energy, and a willingness to do what it takes to fit exercise into their schedules.

49. **A) is correct.** The tone of the letter is cordial. The letter uses mostly friendly and supportive words in a professional format. The chief begins his letter by applauding employees for wanting to meet standards. He clearly explains the reasoning for his own choices in changing policy by taking away food options and prohibiting exercise on meal breaks. While it is debatable whether those choices are good policy for the officers, the tone of the letter is not angry or overbearing, ruling out choice B. He does express enthusiasm for the "warriors" he already works out with and says they would "love" other officers to join them, but this is more enthusiastic than overbearing, ruling out choice C.

50. **C) is correct.** The introduction to the passage states that most officers spend fifteen hours a day working and commuting. There are twenty-four hours in a day; fifteen subtracted from twenty-four leaves nine hours remaining.

51. **B) is correct.** The author's main point is that witnesses can be unreliable. In paragraph 1, the author states that "the information officers receive is often inaccurate either because the individual was mistaken in his or her perception, was biased, or was purposefully deceptive."

52. **C) is correct.** Dishonesty and mistaken perception are mentioned in the passage as problems with witness reliability.

53. **B) is correct.** In paragraph 3, the author writes, "[w]hile some people have biases they are aware of, sometimes people have biases they are unaware of for a number of reasons." People are generally unaware of the bias they hold.

54. **C) is correct.** Paragraph 2 describes auditory occlusion as "a temporary loss or lessening of hearing; sounds are muted or unheard."

55. **C) is correct.** *Anomaly* means abnormality. In the passage, a *time anomaly* is an abnormality in experiencing time.

56. **B) is correct.** *Blatant* means flagrant. Answer choice A, *obvious*, is close in meaning but is not the *best* answer, because it lacks the negative connotation of flagrant.

57. **A) is correct.** The passage implies that officers must diligently investigate due to witness unreliability. The author states in paragraph 1 that officers "must rely on... statements from witnesses and involved parties...to draw conclusions about what actually occurred" during a crime, making choice B incorrect. Choice C is incorrect because that passage states in paragraph 2 that the "most frequent type of unreliable information is mistaken perception," not individual bias.

58. **A) is correct.** The bulk of the passage is dedicated to showing that conventional wisdom about "fewer calories in than calories out" isn't true for many people and is more complicated than previously believed.

59. **C) is correct.** The author cites several scientific studies to support the argument.

60. **C) is correct.** People misreporting the amount of food they ate would introduce error into studies on weight loss and might make the studies the author cites unreliable.

# PRACTICE TEST TWO

## WRITING

### Grammar

Read the sentence, decide whether it is grammatically correct or incorrect, then choose the correct answer.

1. The Mammoth-Flint Ridge Cave System, located in central Kentucky inside Mammoth Cave National Park, are the largest cave system in the world.
   A) Correct
   B) Incorrect

2. The field of child development are concerned with the emotional, psychological, and biological development of infants and children.
   A) Correct
   B) Incorrect

3. Tropical rain forests are made up of many layers, each of which has its own distinct species.
   A) Correct
   B) Incorrect

4. Some species of fish use luminescent lures to trick other fish into moving closer to them.
   A) Correct
   B) Incorrect

5. Though organized firefighting groups existed as early as ancient Egypt, the first fully state-run brigade was created by Emperor Augustus of Rome and also functioned as the nation's official police force.
   A) Correct
   B) Incorrect

6. In the fight against obesity, countries around the world are imposing taxes on sodas and other sugary drinks in hopes of curbing unhealthy habits.
   A) Correct
   B) Incorrect

7. My sister and my best friend lives in Chicago.
   A) Correct
   B) Incorrect

8. My parents or my brother is going to pick me up from the airport.
   A) Correct
   B) Incorrect

9. The storm chasers, who emphasized the importance of caution in his work, decided not to go out when the rain made visibility too low.

   A) Correct

   B) Incorrect

10. Every officer are going to attend the gala.

    A) Correct

    B) Incorrect

## Clarity

Read the sentence, then review the alternatives to the portion that is italicized. Choose the one that fits the sentence's context and is most clearly stated.

11. Eagerly awaiting time off, *Ebony's vacation was just about to start.*

    A) Ebony's vacation was just about to start.

    B) Ebony's vacation was on the verge of beginning.

    C) Ebony was just about to start her vacation.

12. Greg's neighbor has a dog *which barks all hours of the day and night.*

    A) which barks all hours of the day and night.

    B) that barks all hours of the day and night.

    C) who barks all hours of the day and night.

13. The bus driver lost control of the bus *while turning a corner too fast.*

    A) while turning a corner too fast.

    B) while turning a corner at a high rate of speed.

    C) while he was turning a corner too fast.

14. Officer Daryn said he did not like to drive in pursuits *because the fast speeds make you sick.*

    A) because the fast speeds make you sick.

    B) because the fast speeds make him sick.

    C) because the fast speeds are sickening.

15. Jake and Ronald were playing cards *when Ronald shot Jake in the leg.*

    A) when Ronald shot Jake in the leg.

    B) when he shot him in the leg.

    C) when he was shot in the leg.

16. Generally, most people remain unaware of the judicial system's process *unless they become a party to an action.*

    A) unless they become a party to an action.

    B) unless they are joined to an action through a party.

    C) until they are connected to an action.

17. Detective Sherman *almost got convictions for every felony arrest he ever made.*

    A) almost got convictions for every felony arrest he ever made.

    B) was almost convicted for every felony arrest he ever made.

    C) got convictions for almost every felony arrest he ever made.

18. Family law courtrooms are among the most dangerous *because emotions run high when dealing with family issues.*

    A) because emotions run high when dealing with family issues.

    B) because of emotions running high when people are dealing with family issues.

    C) because of heightened emotions around family issues.

19. Staff members were annoyed *when their bosses would not stop talking.*

    A) when their bosses would not stop talking.

    B) if their bosses would not stop talking.

    C) because their bosses would not stop talking.

**20.** Motorists driving under the influence will be prosecuted *under the fullest extent of the law.*

   **A)** under the fullest extent of the law.

   **B)** to the fullest extent of the law.

   **C)** against the fullest extent of the law.

## Detail

In the following sentence pairs, identify the sentence that has the most detailed and useful information.

**21.**

   **A)** Officer Brenner is conducting a routine patrol of a neighborhood where a string of burglaries has recently taken place. She notices that a suspicious-looking man wearing dark clothing matches the description of the man reported to be involved in the burglaries. The man is moving quickly past her patrol car, refusing to make eye contact and staring at the ground.

   **B)** Officer Brenner is conducting a routine patrol of Southside Place, where a string of burglaries has occurred from April through June. She notices a suspicious-looking Caucasian male, medium build, approximately 25 – 30 years old, wearing a dark hooded sweatshirt and dark pants. He matches the description of the man reported to be involved in the burglaries. The man is moving quickly past her patrol car, staring at the ground.

**22.**

   **A)** On Thursday, January 31, Officer Wright interviewed a witness who described a man breaking into the Southview Convenience Store at 7609 Broadway at approximately 11:30 p.m. the night before. The witness described the suspect as a short man weighing approximately 175 pounds, with long blond hair, wearing a black suit coat.

   **B)** Officer Wright interviewed a witness who described a man breaking into the Southview Convenience Store. The break-in happened on Wednesday, January 30, and the interview occurred the next day. According to the witness, he was short and of medium build. He was wearing a black suit coat and had long blond hair.

**23.**

   **A)** On Saturday, September 4, at 1:43 a.m., Officer Yarborough initiated a traffic stop on a brown sedan with a broken taillight at 887 Round Ridge Lane. The driver of the sedan refused to stop, driving away at a high speed.

   **B)** In a suburban neighborhood, Officer Yarborough initiated a traffic stop on a brown sedan with a broken taillight. The traffic stop occurred on September 4, a Saturday night. The driver of the sedan refused to stop and sped away from the patrol car.

**24.**

   **A)** Officer Hernandez is patrolling a rural area at approximately 8:30 p.m. on Thursday, October 23, when he notices a motorcycle driving recklessly, swerving from left to right on a paved country road. The motorcycle is a red Ducati with a Michigan license plate that says REV-1819.

   **B)** Officer Hernandez observed a motorcycle driving recklessly at approximately 8:30 p.m. on Thursday, October 23, on Rural Route 90 near Highway 60. He identified the motorcycle as a red Ducati with Michigan plate numbers REV-1819.

25.

- A) Officer Wagoner responded to a noise complaint call at 56 Evergreen Drive on August 3 at 11:43 p.m. The officer hears very loud music playing from the house and observes several cars in the driveway. The neighbors ask for a citation to be issued.
- B) Officer Wagoner responded to a noise complaint call on a Saturday night. The reporting party claims that the people living across the street are playing music too loudly after hours. They ask for a citation to be issued because the neighbor is violating local ordinances.

26.

- A) On Wednesday, Officer Luna received a report of indecent exposure near Lakeside Drive. The suspect is a Caucasian male of medium build and middle-aged. The alleged perpetrator is said to be partially bald, about 52, and wearing a leather jacket.
- B) Officer Luna interviewed a witness who described a man believed to have committed indecent exposure near Lakeside Drive on Wednesday, July 15, at approximately 1:30 p.m. The suspect is a Caucasian male, 50 – 55 years old, approximately five foot eight inches tall and 220 pounds, partially bald, and wearing a leather jacket.

27.

- A) In October 2018, eight armed robberies were committed between the 1800 and 2400 blocks of Capital Avenue. Based on descriptions given by eyewitnesses, the armed robberies are believed to have been carried out by the same person: an African American woman in her late twenties or early thirties. The suspect is about five foot nine, weighs about 180 pounds, and wears sleeveless shirts. She has a large tattoo on her forearm that says "Destiny."
- B) Last fall, several armed robberies were committed on Capital Avenue. Based on descriptions given by eyewitnesses, the armed robberies are believed to have been carried out by the same person. Police officers were provided with the following description: The suspect is an African American woman. She is about five foot nine and weighs about 180 pounds. She is known to wear sleeveless shirts. She has a large tattoo on her forearm that says "Destiny."

## Word Usage

The following questions provide two word choices to complete the sentences below. Choose the word that makes the most sense based on the context of the sentence.

28. Forensics experts noted the kitchen floor was covered in _____ at the crime scene.

    A) flour
    B) flower

29. Kathy was injured when Mike pushed her down the _____ and broke her arm.

    A) stairs
    B) stares

30. A bullet struck Officer Talbot in her _____, and she could not walk for some time.

    A) heal
    B) heel

31. The officers asked the teens to _____ out their alcoholic beverage.

    A) poor
    B) pour

70   Elissa Simon ■ MCOLES Study Guide

**32.** The fire burned _____ homes, a shop, and part of the school.
  **A)** two
  **B)** too

**33.** The suspect has a medium build and _____ purple hair.
  **A)** died
  **B)** dyed

**34.** A true leader must take the _____ of any complicated situation.
  **A)** reigns
  **B)** reins

**35.** Officers are not _____ to take more than four weeks of vacation time a year.
  **A)** allowed
  **B)** aloud

**36.** Without a proper chain of evidence, we could _____ the case.
  **A)** lose
  **B)** loose

**37.** The research organization includes members _____ fields of study span many disciplines, such as math, sciences, arts, humanities, public affairs, and business.
  **A)** whose
  **B)** who's

**38.** There were _____ cars this morning in the parking lot than usual.
  **A)** less
  **B)** fewer

**39.** Growing up, Hank Schrader was my _____, so I decided to join law enforcement.
  **A)** idle
  **B)** idol

**40.** "_____ me that report immediately," shouted Captain Stone.
  **A)** Bring
  **B)** Take

**41.** A large _____ of money was missing from the evidence locker.
  **A)** number
  **B)** amount

**42.** We charged the man with disturbing the _____ when he refused to turn down his music.
  **A)** piece
  **B)** peace

**43.** The officers offered _____ support to the crying victim.
  **A)** there
  **B)** their

## Spelling

Read the following sentences and choose the correct spelling of the missing word.

**44.** Officer Sasser knew the importance of attention to detail and never performed her duties in a _____ manner.
  **A)** perfunctary
  **B)** perfunctory
  **C)** perfunctery

**45.** Sovereign citizens are people who belong to a _____ organization and refuse to recognize the authority of the United States.
  **A)** seditious
  **B)** siditious
  **C)** saditious

46. The president of the neighborhood watch called the police and requested a house be placed under _____ because its occupants were suspected of drug dealing.

    A) survailance
    B) surveillance
    C) survielance

47. Stella survived her attack because she was _____.

    A) tenacious
    B) tinasious
    C) tenasious

48. Ed was arrested for _____ because he was drunk and sleeping on a park bench at two o'clock in the afternoon.

    A) vagrency
    B) vagrancy
    C) vagrincy

49. Sasha filed a restraining order against her ex-boyfriend because he was _____ her at work.

    A) herassing
    B) harassing
    C) harrassing

50. Pursuant to federal and state laws, all jails and prisons make reasonable _____ for inmates who have disabilities to ensure they have the same or comparable access as inmates who do not have disabilities.

    A) accommodations
    B) accomodations
    C) accommadations

51. Bystanders were _____ upset after witnessing such a horrific accident.

    A) noticeably
    B) noticably
    C) noticeibly

52. Jason was arrested because he was in _____ of stolen property.

    A) posession
    B) possession
    C) possesion

53. The River City Police Department found itself under _____ after an officer, who was chasing a dangerous criminal, crashed his patrol car into a storefront during business hours.

    A) siege
    B) seige
    C) segie

54. At his sentencing, Jim _____ apologized for his role in the home invasion robbery.

    A) publicly
    B) pubicly
    C) pulbicly

55. People who are under the influence of certain drugs can become stronger, more unpredictable, and more _____ than an average person.

    A) agressive
    B) aggresive
    C) aggressive

56. Andrea worked long hours as a court reporter and often suffered headaches from extended exposure to _____ lighting.

    A) flowerescent
    B) fluorescent
    C) flourescent

57. The relationship of the prosecution and the defense is _____ by design.

    A) advercerial
    B) advirsareal
    C) adversarial

**58.** The judge ruled the information was not _____ to the case and was thus inadmissible.

   A) germane
   B) germain
   C) gourmain

**59.** We wanted to order extra _____ with our meal.

   A) fries
   B) frys
   C) frees

**60.** The report should be of the highest _____.

   A) cuality
   B) qualitie
   C) quality

# READING

Read each paragraph or passage and choose the response that best answers the question. All questions are self-contained and use only information provided in the passage that precedes them.

These days, it is harder than ever for kids to simply "walk away" from a bully. Bullying among children and adolescents has evolved beyond taunting a smaller or less popular kid while he or she is at school, to cyberstalking children across city and state lines with the use of common electronic devices. Because of the increasing reach of bullies, among other things, suicides and violent confrontations among youth have risen over the years.

Because of the current scope of bullying, school administrators no longer rely solely on teachers to keep kids safe while at school. Rather, administrators build teams of collaborators that include health care workers, teachers, administration, security staff, and law enforcement personnel to ensure schools remain a safe place for kids to learn. School resource officers (SROs) receive training in issues that are unique to youth. Generally, SROs have an office on campus. They are stationed at the school and spend their time dealing with law enforcement issues. They also spend a great deal of time talking to kids about anything that interests them, such as school activities, sports, law enforcement, and life in general. Since SROs talk to kids at particular schools regularly, officers are in a unique position to identify emerging issues and prevent them before they develop into greater problems.

SROs play a large role in managing situations that involve bullying so that *all* involved students and families are heard and respected.

1. Which fact, if true, strengthens the author's main point?

    A) More kids are bullied currently than in previous years.

    B) The majority of bullying happens on school grounds.

    C) Funding for school resource officers has been reduced.

2. According to the passage, why has bullying become so prevalent?

    A) increased negative behavior

    B) school resource officers on school grounds

    C) technological advancement

3. According to the passage, why are SROs important for managing bullying?

    A) SROs arrest students who are too aggressive.

    B) SROs get to know students and can prevent problems.

    C) SROs provide defensive training for victims of bullies.

Credit scores, which range from 300 to 850, are a single value that summarizes an individual's credit history. Pay your bills late? Your credit score will be lower than someone who gets that electric bill filed on the first of every month. Just paid off your massive student loans? You can expect your credit score to shoot up. The companies that compile credit scores actually keep track of all the loans, credit cards, and bill payments in your name. This massive amount of information is summed up in a credit report, which is then distilled to a single value: your credit score.

Credit scores are used by many institutions that need to evaluate the risk of providing loans, rentals, or services to individuals. Banks use credit scores when deciding whether to hand out loans; they can also use them to determine the terms of the loan itself. Similarly, car dealers, landlords, and credit card companies will likely all access your credit report before agreeing to do business with you. Even your employer can access a modified version of your credit report (although it will not have your actual credit score on it).

When it comes to credit, everyone begins with a clean slate. The first time you access any credit—be it a credit card, student loan, or rental agreement—information begins to accumulate in your credit report. Thus, having no credit score can often be just as bad as having a low one. Lenders want to know that you have a history of borrowing money and paying it back on time. After all, if you've never taken out a loan, how can a bank know that you'll pay back its money? So, having nothing on your credit report can result in low credit limits and high interest rates.

With time, though, credit scores can be raised. With every payment, your credit report improves and banks will be more likely to loan you money. These new loans will in turn raise your score even further (as long as you keep making payments, of course).

In general, you can take a number of basic steps to raise your credit score. First, ensure that payments are made on time. When payments are past due, it not only has a negative impact on your score, but new creditors will be reluctant to lend while you are delinquent on other accounts.

Being smart about taking on debt is another key factor in keeping your credit score high. As someone who is just starting off in the financial world, there will be multiple offers to open accounts, say, for an introductory credit card or short-term loan. You may also find that as your score increases, you will receive offers for larger and larger loans. (Predatory lenders are a scourge on the young as well as the old.) But just because banks are offering you those loans doesn't make them a good idea. Instead, you should only take on debt you know you can pay back in a reasonable amount of time.

Lastly, keep an eye on unpaid student loans, medical bills, and parking tickets, all of which can take a negative toll on your credit score. In fact, your credit score will take a major hit from any bill that's sent to a collection agency, so it's in your best interest to avoid letting bills get to that point. Many organizations will agree to keep bills away from collection agencies if you set up a fee payment system.

4. What is the author's primary purpose in writing this essay?
   A) to help readers understand and improve their credit scores
   B) to warn banks about the dangers of lending to people with no credit score
   C) to persuade readers to take out large loans to improve their credit scores

5. According to the passage, which individual is likely to have the highest credit score?
   A) someone who has had medical bills sent to a collection agency
   B) someone who is in the process of paying back their student loans
   C) someone who has borrowed a large amount of money and paid it back on time

6. What is the meaning of the word *distilled* in the first paragraph?
   A) to refine to its essence
   B) to explain at length
   C) to keep records of

7. What is the best summary of this passage?
   A) Individuals with low credit scores will likely have trouble getting credit cards and loans. However, they can improve their credit scores over time.
   B) Having no credit score can often be worse than having a low credit score, so it's important to sign up for credit cards and loans early in life.
   C) Credit scores summarize an individual's credit history and are used by many businesses. They can be improved by making smart financial decisions.

8. Which of the following is an opinion stated in the passage?
   A) Credit scores, which range from 300 to 850, are a single value that summarizes an individual's credit history.
   B) Predatory lenders are a scourge on the young as well as the old.
   C) After all, if you've never taken out a loan, how can a bank know that you'll pay back its money?

9. What can the reader conclude from the passage?

   A) It's possible to wipe your credit report clean and start over with a blank slate.

   B) People with a large amount of debt can likely get a loan with a low interest rate because they have demonstrated they are trustworthy.

   C) Someone who has borrowed and paid back large sums of money will get a loan with more favorable terms than someone who has never borrowed money before.

10. Which statement is NOT a detail from the passage?

    A) In general, you can take a number of basic steps to raise your credit score.

    B) When it comes to credit, everyone begins with a clean slate.

    C) Employers can access your credit score before hiring you.

---

(1)

After a person convicted of a crime has served a sentence in a jail or prison, he or she is released back into the community. Prisoner release is a source of relief or frustration depending on individual perceptions, experience, and expectations. Some people believe a person who has committed a crime is lost and can never be <u>redeemed</u>. Others believe there are justifiable reasons why any given crime was committed, and thus very few people should go to jail or prison for extended times. Regardless of one's position, when a person has served a sentence, that individual will be released and will return to the community. Moreover, regardless of the opinions of others, the released person often has to deal with fear, confusion, and apprehension.

(2)

So there are many questions that arise. Is it the responsibility of the community to support people who have violated the public trust as they re-enter society? And if so, how do communities support people newly released from jail so they do not become a statistic of recidivism? The answer to these questions forms the basis of re-entry programs throughout the nation.

(3)

Generally speaking, most re-entry programs are composed of various community members and stakeholders. Collaboration between probation, parole, law enforcement, medical and mental health care workers, employment services, housing advocates, clergy, and a host of other services including substance abuse and domestic violence counseling are essential for making the transition smooth and successful. Collaborative partners ensure that resources are set up, or in motion, by the time of release so that participants do not find themselves homeless or re-entering a detrimental living situation immediately upon leaving prison.

(4)

Re-entry programs have shown success in many communities. However, the perceived level of success may be well above or well below expectations, depending on individual <u>disposition</u>, the attitude of the participant, and the community in which they now live.

---

11. Based on the passage, it can be inferred that the author believes which of the following?

    A) Criminals should never be let out of prison.

    B) Many crimes are justified, and fewer people should receive long prison terms.

    C) Community involvement is important for re-entry programs to work well.

12. What is an appropriate title for this passage?

    A) Community Frustrated Over Prisoner Release

    B) Prisoner Re-entry Programs: What Happens Next

    C) How to Decrease Recidivism Rates

13. Based on the tone of this passage, which is it meant to do?

    A) persuade
    B) share information
    C) stimulate thought

14. As used in the last sentence, what is the best definition of the word *disposition*?

    A) bad attitude
    B) frustrations
    C) natural inclination

15. What is the purpose of the second paragraph?

    A) to illustrate the depth of the issue
    B) to offer a supporting example
    C) to avoid taking a position

16. Which is the best synonym for the word *redeemed* as used in paragraph 1?

    A) exchanged
    B) converted
    C) reformed

In recent decades, jazz has been associated with New Orleans and festivals like Mardi Gras, but in the 1920s, jazz was a booming trend whose influence reached into many aspects of American culture. In fact, the years between World War I and the Great Depression were known as the Jazz Age, a term coined by F. Scott Fitzgerald in his famous novel *The Great Gatsby*. Sometimes also called the Roaring Twenties, this time period saw major urban centers experiencing new economic, cultural, and artistic vitality. In the United States, musicians flocked to cities like New York and Chicago, which would become famous hubs for jazz musicians. Ella Fitzgerald, for example, moved from Virginia to New York City to begin her much-lauded singing career, and jazz pioneer Louis Armstrong got his big break in Chicago.

Jazz music was played by and for a more expressive and freed populace than the United States had previously seen. Women gained the right to vote and were openly seen drinking and dancing to jazz music. This period marked the emergence of the flapper, a woman determined to make a statement about her new role in society. Jazz music also provided the soundtrack for the explosion of African American art and culture now known as the Harlem Renaissance. In addition to Fitzgerald and Armstrong, numerous musicians, including Duke Ellington, Fats Waller, and Bessie Smith, promoted their distinctive and complex music as an integral part of the emerging African American culture.

17. What is the main idea of the passage?

    A) People should associate jazz music with the 1920s, not modern New Orleans.
    B) Jazz music played an important role in many cultural movements of the 1920s.
    C) Many famous jazz musicians began their careers in New York City and Chicago.

18. What is a reasonable inference that can be drawn from this passage?

    A) Jazz music was important to minority groups struggling for social equality in the 1920s.
    B) Duke Ellington, Fats Waller, and Bessie Smith were the most important jazz musicians of the Harlem Renaissance.
    C) Women gained the right to vote with the help of jazz musicians.

19. What is the author's primary purpose in writing this essay?

    A) to explain the role jazz musicians played in the Harlem Renaissance
    B) to inform the reader about the many important musicians playing jazz in the 1920s
    C) to discuss how jazz influenced important cultural movements in the 1920s

20. What can the reader conclude from the passage above?

    A) F. Scott Fitzgerald supported jazz musicians in New York and Chicago.
    B) Jazz music is no longer as popular as it once was.
    C) Both women and African Americans used jazz music as a way of expressing their newfound freedom.

**21.** Which of the following is NOT a fact stated in the passage?

- **A)** The years between World War I and the Great Depression were known as the Jazz Age.
- **B)** Ella Fitzgerald and Louis Armstrong both moved to New York City to start their music careers.
- **C)** Women danced to jazz music during the 1920s to make a statement about their role in society.

---

Taking a person's temperature is one of the most basic and common health care tasks. Everyone from nurses to emergency medical technicians to concerned parents should be able to grab a thermometer to take a patient or loved one's temperature. But what's the best way to get an accurate reading? The answer depends on the situation.

The most common way people measure body temperature is orally. A simple digital or disposable thermometer is placed under the tongue for a few minutes, and the task is done. There are many situations, however, when measuring temperature orally isn't an option. For example, when a person can't breathe through his nose, he won't be able to keep his mouth closed long enough to get an accurate reading. In these situations, it's often preferable to place the thermometer in the rectum or armpit. Using the rectum also has the added benefit of providing a much more accurate reading than other locations can provide.

It's also often the case that certain people, like agitated patients or fussy babies, won't be able to sit still long enough for an accurate reading. In these situations, it's best to use a thermometer that works much more quickly, such as one that measures temperature in the ear or at the temporal artery. No matter which method is chosen, however, it's important to check the average temperature for each region, as it can vary by several degrees.

---

**22.** What is the best summary of this passage?

- **A)** It's important that everyone know the best way to take a person's temperature in any given situation.
- **B)** The most common method of taking a person's temperature—orally—isn't appropriate in some situations.
- **C)** The most accurate way to take a temperature is placing a digital thermometer in the rectum.

**23.** What is the meaning of the word *agitated* in the last paragraph?

- **A)** obviously upset
- **B)** quickly moving
- **C)** violently ill

**24.** According to the passage, why is it sometimes preferable to take a person's temperature rectally?

- **A)** Rectal readings are more accurate than oral readings.
- **B)** Many people cannot sit still long enough to have their temperatures taken orally.
- **C)** Temperature readings can vary widely between regions of the body.

**25.** Which statement is NOT a detail from the passage?

- **A)** Taking a temperature in the ear or at the temporal artery is more accurate than taking it orally.
- **B)** If an individual cannot breathe through the nose, taking his or her temperature orally will likely give an inaccurate reading.
- **C)** The standard human body temperature varies depending on whether it's measured in the mouth, rectum, armpit, ear, or at the temporal artery.

**26.** What is the author's primary purpose in writing this essay?

- **A)** to advocate for the use of thermometers that measure temperature in the ear or at the temporal artery
- **B)** to explain the methods available to measure a person's temperature and the situation where each method is appropriate
- **C)** to warn readers that the average temperature of the human body varies by region

Skin coloration and markings have an important role to play in the world of snakes. Those intricate diamonds, stripes, and swirls help the animals hide from predators, but perhaps most importantly (for us humans, anyway), the markings can also indicate whether the snake is venomous. While it might seem counterintuitive for a venomous snake to stand out in bright red or blue, that fancy costume tells any nearby predator that approaching him would be a bad idea.

If you see a flashy-looking snake in the woods, though, those markings don't necessarily mean it's venomous: some snakes have found a way to ward off predators without the actual venom. The scarlet kingsnake, for example, has very similar markings to the venomous coral snake with whom it frequently shares a habitat. However, the kingsnake is actually nonvenomous; it's merely pretending to be dangerous to eat. A predatory hawk or eagle, usually hunting from high in the sky, can't tell the difference between the two species, and so the kingsnake gets passed over and lives another day.

27. What is the author's primary purpose in writing this essay?

    A) to explain how the markings on a snake are related to whether it's venomous

    B) to teach readers the difference between coral snakes and kingsnakes

    C) to illustrate why snakes are dangerous

28. What can the reader conclude from the passage above?

    A) The kingsnake is dangerous to humans.

    B) The coral snake and the kingsnake are both hunted by the same predators.

    C) It's safe to handle snakes in the woods because you can easily tell whether they're poisonous.

29. What is the best summary of this passage?

    A) Humans can use coloration and markings on snakes to determine whether they're venomous.

    B) Animals often use coloration to hide from predators.

    C) Venomous snakes often have bright markings, although nonvenomous snakes can also mimic those colors.

30. Which statement is NOT a detail from the passage?

    A) Predators will avoid eating kingsnakes because their markings are similar to those on coral snakes.

    B) Kingsnakes and coral snakes live in the same habitats.

    C) The coral snake uses its coloration to hide from predators.

31. What is the meaning of the word *intricate* in the first paragraph?

    A) complex

    B) colorful

    C) purposeful

32. What is the difference between kingsnakes and coral snakes according to the passage?

    A) Both kingsnakes and coral snakes are nonvenomous, but coral snakes have colorful markings.

    B) Both kingsnakes and coral snakes are venomous, but kingsnakes have colorful markings.

    C) Kingsnakes are nonvenomous while coral snakes are venomous.

It could be said that the great battle between the North and South we call the Civil War was a battle for individual identity. The states of the South had their own culture, one based on farming, independence, and the rights of both man and state to determine their own paths. Similarly, the North had forged its own identity as a center of centralized commerce and manufacturing. This clash of lifestyles was bound to create tension, and this tension was bound to lead to war. But people who try to sell you this narrative are wrong. The Civil War was not a battle of cultural identities—it was a battle about slavery. All other explanations for the war are either a direct consequence of the South's desire for wealth at the expense of her fellow man or a fanciful invention to cover up this sad portion of our nation's history. And it cannot be denied that this time in our past was very sad indeed.

33. What is the meaning of the word *fanciful* in the passage?

    A) complicated

    B) imaginative

    C) successful

34. What is the main idea of the passage?

    A) The Civil War was the result of cultural differences between the North and South.

    B) The Civil War was caused by the South's reliance on slave labor.

    C) The North's use of commerce and manufacturing allowed it to win the war.

35. What is the author's primary purpose in writing this essay?

    A) to convince readers that slavery was the main cause of the Civil War

    B) to illustrate the cultural differences between the North and the South before the Civil War

    C) to persuade readers that the North deserved to win the Civil War

In its most basic form, geography is the study of space; more specifically, it studies the physical space of the earth and the ways in which it interacts with, shapes, and is shaped by its habitants. Geographers look at the world from a spatial perspective. This means that at the center of all geographic study is the question, *where?* For geographers, the *where* of any interaction, event, or development is a crucial element to understanding it.

This question of *where* can be asked in a variety of fields of study, so there are many sub-disciplines of geography. These can be organized into four main categories: 1) regional studies, which examine the characteristics of a particular place; 2) topical studies, which look at a single physical or human feature that impacts the whole world; 3) physical studies, which focus on the physical features of Earth; and 4) human studies, which examine the relationship between human activity and the environment.

36. A researcher studying the relationship between farming and river systems would be engaged in which of the following geographical sub-disciplines?

    A) regional studies

    B) topical studies

    C) human studies

37. Which of the following best describes the mode of the passage?

    A) expository

    B) narrative

    C) persuasive

38. Which of the following is a concise summary of the passage?

    A) The most important questions in geography are where an event or development took place.

    B) Geography, which is the study of the physical space on Earth, can be broken down into four sub-disciplines.

    C) Regional studies is the study of a single region or area.

Sweat glands can be found all over the body. They lie beneath the skin and help regulate body temperature by transporting water to the skin's surface. The most common type of sweat glands are eccrine glands. They are tiny, coiled glands and are concentrated on the palm of your hand and the sole of your foot. There are about two million to five million eccrine glands in the body, with about four hundred to five hundred per square centimeter in the palm of your hand. These glands are controlled by the sympathetic nervous system, which stimulates perspiration. The sweat that pours out of these glands is normally colorless and odorless.

Body odor tends to form around a special type of sweat gland—the apocrine glands—which develop in human beings during puberty. They are located in the armpits and in the groin. They, too, emit odorless perspiration, but bacteria in these areas mix with the apocrine secretions to create body odor.

Mammary glands are specialized examples of apocrine glands. Mammary glands produce milk following the birth of a child. Thus, sweat glands are not only associated with perspiration, but also lactation.

**39.** According to the passage, what is one specialized type of apocrine gland?

   **A)** sweat glands

   **B)** glands in the hands and feet

   **C)** mammary glands

**40.** Readers can infer that most people do not know that mammary glands

   **A)** are a type of sweat gland.

   **B)** is a term that is related to the word *mammal*.

   **C)** produce milk for nursing babies.

**41.** What is the author's primary purpose in writing these paragraphs?

   **A)** to inform readers about types and functions of sweat glands

   **B)** to persuade readers to practice good hygiene

   **C)** to inform readers about the sympathetic nervous system

Chronic traumatic encephalopathy (CTE) is a degenerative brain disease that has garnered the attention of the media in recent years. Medical studies have indicated that American football players have a higher chance of developing CTE than many other athletes because of the repeated brain trauma that results from helmet-to-helmet collisions on the field. Some studies have found that nearly 87 percent of all football players show signs of CTE. This is a troubling statistic, considering that CTE has been linked to memory loss, mood disorders, and even dementia. There is also a strong correlation with CTE and suicide, and it may be the high percentage of suicides among former NFL players that has shed light on the troubling symptoms of chronic head trauma.

Many organizations, colleges, and high schools have responded by introducing stricter standards for concussion protocols and head-to-head collisions. However, even these protocols have done little to mitigate the traumatic consequences of accidental helmet-to-helmet collisions that occur on a daily basis on football fields across the country. Many concerned parents have begun to ask if football is too violent a sport for their children. It may be too early for Americans to honestly answer this question, but there is certainly room for growing concern. Recent statistics show a decline in enrollment in youth football programs across the country, and for good reason: head trauma—no matter how many times or how often—appears to have long-term effects on the brain and the mind.

**42.** Which sentence best summarizes the passage's main idea?

   **A)** CTE is a degenerative brain disease that a large percentage of American football players develop.

   **B)** CTE has been linked to memory loss, mood disorders, dementia, and suicide among former NFL players.

   **C)** Many organizations, colleges, and high schools have introduced stricter standards for concussion protocols and head-to-head collisions.

**43.** Which of the following is NOT listed as a detail in the passage?

   **A)** Studies have shown that American football players have a higher chance of developing CTE than other athletes do.

   **B)** When playing football, players sustain repeated brain trauma from helmet-to-helmet collisions.

   **C)** Professional football organizations across the United States are taking responsibility for the high incidence of CTE among players.

**44.** Readers can infer from reading this passage that professional football's future

A) may be threatened.

B) will not be affected by CTE studies.

C) will definitely be threatened.

**45.** In the second paragraph, the author writes, "It may be too early for Americans to honestly answer this question, but there is certainly room for growing concern." To which question does the author refer?

A) Is playing professional football worth suffering memory loss, mood disorders, and dementia?

B) Should football fans stop attending games and watching football on television?

C) Is tackle football too violent a sport for children?

**46.** What is the meaning of the word *garnered* in the first sentence?

A) harvested

B) gotten

C) stored

**47.** What is the author's primary purpose in writing this essay?

A) to reassure readers that football players' brains can heal from CTE

B) to suggest that, following any kind of head trauma, an athlete should take several months off to heal

C) to suggest that football may be too violent a sport for children and teenagers to play

---

The greatest changes in sensory, motor, and perceptual development happen in the first two years of life. When babies are first born, most of their senses operate in a similar way to those of adults. For example, babies are able to hear before they are born; studies show that babies turn toward the sound of their mothers' voices just minutes after being born, indicating they recognize the mother's voice from their time in the womb.

The exception to this rule is vision. A baby's vision changes significantly in its first year of life; initially it has a range of vision of only 8 – 12 inches and no depth perception. As a result, infants rely primarily on hearing; vision does not become the dominant sense until around the age of twelve months. Babies also prefer faces to other objects. This preference, along with their limited vision range, means that their sight is initially focused on their caregiver.

---

**48.** According to the passage, which of the following senses do babies primarily rely on?

A) vision

B) hearing

C) touch

**49.** Which of the following best describes the mode of the passage?

A) expository

B) narrative

C) persuasive

**50.** Which of the following is a concise summary of the passage?

A) Babies have no depth perception until twelve months, which is why they focus only on their caregivers' faces.

B) Babies can recognize their mothers' voices when born, so they initially rely primarily on their sense of hearing.

C) Babies have senses similar to those of adults except for their sense of sight, which doesn't fully develop until twelve months.

---

Studies by the American Medical Association and the American Cancer Society link the prevalence of over a dozen types of cancer to smoking cigarettes: colon cancer, pancreatic cancer, kidney cancer, liver cancer, stomach cancer, throat cancer, lung cancer, and leukemia, among others, are believed to be related to heavy tobacco smoking. Even though cigarette use has been plummeting in the United States, close to 40 million people continue to smoke. This number is troubling, especially when one considers that nearly 30 percent of all cancer-related deaths in the United States can be tied to smoking. To make matters worse, cigarette-linked cancers disproportionately affect men of color, especially if they come from lower-income communities. This means that smoking continues to be not only an issue of public health, but also one of social equity.

Smoking is linked to other health problems as well. Heart disease and stroke are among the most visible, but cigarette smoke affects nearly every organ in the human body. It is correlated with birth defects, lower sperm counts, diabetes, lower bone density, tooth loss and gum disease, and more.

Continuing research reinforces the necessity of anti-smoking campaigns, both government funded and grassroots. The numbers show that such campaigns work, encouraging people to quit smoking. For the moment, however, the United States still has a long road of anti-smoking campaigning ahead.

**51.** Which sentence best summarizes the passage's main idea?

A) "Studies … link the prevalence of over a dozen types of cancer to smoking cigarettes."

B) "Even though cigarette use has been plummeting in the United States, close to 40 million people continue to smoke."

C) "This number [40 million smokers] is troubling, especially when one considers that nearly 30 percent of all cancer-related deaths in the United States can be tied to smoking."

**52.** In the last sentence, what does the phrase "still has a long road … ahead" mean?

A) People should not smoke on public transportation.

B) A cancer patient has a long, grueling treatment program to suffer through.

C) Anti-smoking campaigns still have a lot more work to do in the United States.

**53.** Which phrase from the passage has about the same meaning as "are believed to be related to" in the first paragraph?

A) "can be tied to" (paragraph 1)

B) "disproportionately affect" (paragraph 1)

C) "are among the most visible" (paragraph 2)

**54.** Which of the following is NOT listed as a detail in the passage?

A) The American Medical Association and the American Cancer Society have sponsored studies that show smoking cigarettes causes cancer.

B) Tobacco companies advertise cigarettes on billboards and smaller signs in low-income neighborhoods.

C) Cigarette smoking is also linked to heart disease, strokes, birth defects, and diabetes.

**55.** What is the author's primary purpose in writing this essay?

A) to suggest "the necessity of anti-smoking campaigns"

B) to scare smokers into quitting cigarette smoking immediately

C) to honor the research done by the American Medical Association and the American Cancer Society

**56.** Readers can infer from reading this passage that the author thinks all cigarette smokers

A) are uneducated.

B) should quit smoking.

C) are low-class people.

Empathy is different from mimicry or sympathy—it is neither imitating someone else's emotions nor feeling concern for their suffering. Empathy is much more complex; it is the ability to actually share and comprehend the emotions of others.

Empathy takes on two major forms: cognitive empathy and affective, or emotional, empathy. Cognitive empathy is the ability to identify and understand the emotions, mental state, or perspective of others. Affective empathy is the ability to experience an emotional response to the emotions of others—either to feel what they are feeling or to have an appropriate emotional reaction, such as feeling sad when hearing about someone's bad news. Related to affective empathy is compassionate empathy, the ability to control your own emotions while helping others deal with theirs.

Empathy is crucial for being able to respond properly in social settings. People who suffer from some psychiatric conditions, such as autism spectrum disorder, may struggle with being empathetic. Conversely, some people with very strong cognitive empathy may abuse their social understanding as a means to take advantage of others. Most people, however, choose moments and contexts in which they are likely to relate to the emotions of others.

**57.** What is the author's primary purpose in writing these paragraphs?

**A)** to define empathy

**B)** to persuade readers to show more empathy

**C)** to advise readers about ways to appear empathetic

**58.** According to the passage, what is one negative use of empathy?

**A)** People who actually possess little or no empathy may fake this quality.

**B)** People who are empathetic may feel too much concern for others' suffering.

**C)** People who are able to identify and understand others' emotions, mental state, or perspective may abuse this knowledge by taking advantage of others.

**59.** The reader can infer from the passage that the author believes empathy is

**A)** a primarily positive quality.

**B)** similar to autism spectrum disorder.

**C)** similar to mimicry or sympathy.

**60.** Readers can infer that _____ might be most useful to a medical professional who responds to emergencies.

**A)** sympathy and mimicry

**B)** compassionate empathy

**C)** affective empathy

# ANSWER KEY

## Writing

1. **B) is correct.** This sentence is grammatically incorrect. The verb *are* is conjugated incorrectly. The subject "Mammoth-Flint Ridge Cave System" is singular, so the verb should be singular: *is*.

2. **B) is correct.** This sentence is grammatically incorrect. The verb *are* is conjugated incorrectly. The subject *field* is singular, so the verb should be singular: *is*.

3. **A) is correct.** This sentence is grammatically correct. *Are* is a present-tense plural helping verb describing the actions of the plural subject *rain forests*. The singular verb *has* matches its singular antecedent *each*.

4. **A) is correct.** This sentence is grammatically correct. The present-tense plural verb *use* describes the actions of the plural subject *species*.

5. **A) is correct.** This sentence is grammatically correct. The phrase *and also functioned* introduces the second part of a compound verb phrase: *was created…and…functioned*.

6. **A) is correct.** This sentence is grammatically correct. *Are* is a present-tense plural helping verb describing the actions of the plural subject *countries*.

7. **B) is correct.** This sentence contains an error. The compound subject "My sister and my best friend" requires a plural verb: *live*.

8. **A) is correct.** This sentence is grammatically correct. The verb *is* agrees with the subject closest to it: the singular noun *brother*.

9. **B) is correct.** This sentence contains an error. The singular possessive pronoun *his* should be replaced with the plural possessive *their* to agree with the plural antecedent *storm chasers*.

10. **B) is correct.** This sentence contains an error. The singular subject *officer* does not agree with the plural verb *are*. The verb should be changed to *is*.

11. **C) is correct.** Answers A and B contain a misplaced modifier. The phrase "eagerly awaiting time off" modifies *Ebony's vacation* rather than *Ebony*, making it seem like the vacation, not the person, was waiting for time off.

12. **B) is correct.** There is no comma after *dog*, so the relative pronoun *that* must be used to form a restrictive clause. Both *which* and *who* require commas after *dog* to set off the relative phrase. Also, *who* is not generally used with a nonhuman antecedent.

13. **A) is correct.** Choice A is the most concise; the other choices are too wordy.

14. **B) is correct.** Answer A contains the pronoun *you*, which does not agree with the subject *Officer Daryn*. Choice B uses *him* to clearly state that it is Officer Daryn who gets sick at high speeds. Choice C is too vague; it is not clear what is *sickening* about the fast speeds.

15. **A) is correct.** Choice A is the only one that clearly explains who shot whom in the leg. Although choices B and C are shorter, it is not clear who was shot and who did the shooting.

16. **A) is correct.** Answer A is the most concise and uses the correct preposition: *unless*. Choice B is wordy and unclear. Choice C uses the preposition *until*, which changes the sentence's meaning.

17. **C) is correct.** Answer A contains a misplaced modifier. The phrase "Detective Sherman *almost* got convictions" implies he got acquittals rather than convictions. Choice B completely changes the sentence's meaning, implying that Detective Sherman himself was convicted of crimes. Choice C is the clearest, as the word *almost* modifies *every… arrest*, rather than *convictions*.

18. **C) is correct.** Choice C is the most concise. Choices A and B are wordy.

19. **C) is correct.** Choice C most clearly explains why the staff members were annoyed by using the word *because*.

20. **B) is correct.** Choice B uses the correct preposition, *to*. The other choices use incorrect prepositions, creating unclear and confusing sentences.

21. **B) is correct.** Choice B contains more specific details like the place where the burglaries occurred, the time period they have occurred, and the description of the suspect.

22. **A) is correct.** Choice A contains more details, like the time of the incident and the store's address. It also describes the suspect in more detail. Furthermore, a sentence in choice B contains a pronoun error, making it unclear whether the suspect or the witness is being described.

23. **A) is correct.** Choice A provides the time and exact address of the traffic stop. It also expresses the information more clearly.

24. **B) is correct.** Choice B provides more precise information about the location and is more concisely written. Choice A states that the motorcyclist was "swerving from left to right," which is unnecessary information since the report already states the motorcyclist was "driving recklessly."

25. **A) is correct.** Choice A provides more pertinent information about the time and location of the incident and the officer's observations.

26. **B) is correct.** Choice B provides more details about the time and location of the incident and the suspect's description.

27. **A) is correct.** Choice A contains more pertinent details about the suspect and the armed robberies.

28. **A) is correct.** *Flour* is a white powdery substance made from wheat and used for cooking. A *flower* is a colorful plant with petals.

29. **A) is correct.** *Stairs* refers to steps used to walk from one floor to another. To *stare* is to gaze fixedly for a long period of time.

30. **B) is correct.** The *heel* is the back part of the foot. To *heal* is to get better or become healthy.

31. **B) is correct.** To *pour* is to disperse from a container. *Poor* means "having very little money."

32. **A) is correct.** *Two* describes a quantity of more than one but less than three. *Too* means "in addition" or "also."

33. **B) is correct.** To *dye* is to artificially change color. To *die* is to cease to live.

34. **B) is correct.** *Reins* are the straps that control an animal. The idiomatic expression "take the reins" means to take control of a situation. To *reign* is to rule over, usually a kingdom.

35. **A) is correct.** *Allowed* means permitted or able to. *Aloud* means audible or said out loud.

36. **A) is correct.** To *lose* is to fail to win. *Loose* means "not firmly in place."

37. **A) is correct.** *Whose* is a possessive pronoun referring to the members. *Who's* is a contraction of *who is* or *who has*.

38. **B) is correct.** *Fewer* is used to indicate a smaller amount of something plural (in this case, *cars*). *Less* is used to indicate a smaller amount of something that cannot be counted (for instance, water or air).

39. **B) is correct.** An *idol* is someone to admire or look up to. *Idle* means lazy.

40. **A) is correct.** *Bring* is used to indicate transporting something toward the speaker. *Take* should be used to indicate transporting something away from the speaker.

41. **B) is correct.** An *amount* refers to a noncountable quantity, like money. *Number* refers to a countable quantity (e.g., coins or bills).

42. **B) is correct.** *Peace* refers to calm, quiet, or lack of conflict. A *piece* of something is a portion or part of it.

43. **B) is correct.** *Their* is the possessive pronoun meaning "belonging to them." *There* refers to place or location.

44. **B) is correct.** Choice B, *perfunctory*, is correct.

45. **A) is correct,** *seditious*.

46. **B) is correct,** *surveillance*.

47. **A) is correct,** *tenacious*.

48. **B) is correct,** *vagrancy*.

49. **B) is correct,** *harassing*.

50. **A) is correct,** *accommodations*.

51. **A) is correct,** *noticeably*.

52. **B) is correct,** *possession*.

53. **A) is correct,** *siege*.

54. **A) is correct,** *publicly*.

55. **C) is correct,** *aggressive*.

56. **B) is correct,** *fluorescent*.

57. **C) is correct,** *adversarial*.

58. **A) is correct,** *germane*.

59. **A) is correct,** *fries*.

60. **C) is correct,** *quality*.

# READING

1. **A) is correct.** The author's main point is that bullying has increased in scope from years past. If the number of children being bullied has increased, this strengthens the author's argument.

2. **C) is correct.** The passage immediately asserts that technological advancement has made bullying more prevalent. The first paragraph states that "[b]ullying among children and adolescents has evolved…to cyberstalking children across city and state lines with the use of common electronic devices."

3. **B) is correct.** According to the passage, "SROs talk to kids at particular schools regularly," so "officers are in a unique position to identify emerging issues and prevent them before they develop into greater problems."

4. **A) is correct.** The author provides an overview of the various elements that affect credit scores and offers suggestions about how to improve credit scores.

5. **C) is correct.** The author writes that "[w]ith every payment, your credit report improves and banks will be more likely to loan you money. These new loans will in turn raise your score even further (as long as you keep making payments, of course)." Thus, it can be inferred that someone who has paid off a large amount of money and paid it back in time will have a high credit score.

6. **A) is correct.** In this context, *distilled* refers to the process of creditors taking the "massive amount of information [that] is summed up in a credit report" and converting it into a single value that represents the overall reliability of the potential borrower or renter.

7. **C) is correct.** This statement provides an adequate summary of the passage, as it explains what a credit score is and how individuals can raise their credit scores.

8. **B) is correct.** The word "scourge" is emotional and representative of the author's personal opinion about predatory lenders.

9. **C) is correct.** The author writes that "having nothing on your credit report can result in low credit limits and high interest rates." This implies that someone who has borrowed and paid back a loan on time will likely have higher limits and lower interest rates than someone who has no credit history.

10. **C) is correct.** The author writes that "[e]ven your employer can access a modified version of your credit report (although it will not have your actual credit score on it)."

11. **C) is correct.** Answer C is the best choice because the passage discusses the value of collaboration among community stakeholders.

12. **B) is correct.** Choice B best addresses the ideas of the passage, which discusses the details of reentry programs.

13. **C) is correct.** The main point of the passage is to stimulate thought. It presents a difficult issue: prisoner release. It also addresses two perspectives, noting that "[s]ome people believe a person who has committed a crime is lost and can never be redeemed," while "[o]thers believe there are justifiable reasons why any given crime was committed, and thus very few people should go to jail or prison for extended times." The passage also asks the reader to consider how to support prisoners in the community.

14. **C) is correct.** *Disposition* in this context means "natural inclination" to do something.

15. **A) is correct.** Paragraph 2 provokes the reader into thinking more deeply about prisoner reentry by asking direct questions, illustrating the depth of the issue.

16. **C) is correct.** To *redeem* means to buy back, recover, exchange, or reform. In this context, *redeemed* means "reformed."

17. **B) is correct.** The author writes that "[j]azz music was played by and for a more expressive and freed populace than the United States had previously seen." In addition to

"the emergence of the flapper," the 1920s saw "the explosion of African American art and culture now known as the Harlem Renaissance."

18. **A) is correct.** The author writes that "[j]azz music was played by and for a more expressive and freed populace than the United States had previously seen." In addition to "the emergence of the flapper," the 1920s saw "the explosion of African American art and culture now known as the Harlem Renaissance."

19. **C) is correct.** The author opens the passage saying, "In recent decades, jazz has been associated with New Orleans and festivals like Mardi Gras, but in the 1920s, jazz was a booming trend whose influence reached into many aspects of American culture." He then goes on to elaborate on what these movements were.

20. **C) is correct.** The author writes that "[j]azz music was played by and for a more expressive and freed populace than the United States had previously seen." In addition to "the emergence of the flapper," the 1920s saw "the explosion of African American art and culture now known as the Harlem Renaissance."

21. **B) is correct.** At the end of the first paragraph, the author writes, "Ella Fitzgerald, for example, moved from Virginia to New York City to begin her much-lauded singing career, and jazz pioneer Louis Armstrong got his big break in Chicago."

22. **B) is correct.** The author indicates that the "most common way people measure body temperature is orally" but that "[t]here are many situations…when measuring temperature orally isn't an option." She then goes on to describe these situations in the second and third paragraphs.

23. **A) is correct.** The final paragraph states that "agitated patients…won't be able to sit still long enough for an accurate reading." The reader can infer that an agitated patient is a patient who is visibly upset, annoyed, or uncomfortable.

24. **A) is correct.** The second paragraph of the passage states that "[u]sing the rectum also has the added benefit of providing a much more accurate reading than other locations can provide."

25. **A) is correct.** This detail is not stated in the passage.

26. **B) is correct.** In the first paragraph, the author writes, "But what's the best way to get an accurate reading? The answer depends on the situation." She then goes on to describe various options and their applications.

27. **A) is correct.** The passage indicates that a snakes' "intricate diamonds, stripes, and swirls help the animals hide from predators, but perhaps most importantly (for us humans, anyway), the markings can also indicate whether the snake is venomous."

28. **B) is correct.** The final paragraph of the passage states that the two species "frequently [share] a habitat" and that a "predatory hawk or eagle, usually hunting from high in the sky, can't tell the difference between the two species, and so the kingsnake gets passed over and lives another day."

29. **C) is correct.** This summary captures the main ideas of each paragraph.

30. **C) is correct.** The first paragraph states that "[w]hile it might seem counterintuitive for a venomous snake to stand out in bright red or blue, that fancy costume tells any nearby predator that approaching him would be a bad idea." The coral snake's markings do not allow it to hide from predators but rather to "ward [them] off."

31. **A) is correct.** The passage states that "intricate diamonds, stripes, and swirls help the animals hide from predators," implying that these markings are complex enough to allow the animals to blend in with their surroundings.

32. **C) is correct.** The second paragraph states that the "scarlet kingsnake, for example, has very similar markings to the venomous coral snake with whom it frequently shares

a habitat. However, the kingsnake is actually nonvenomous."

33. **B) is correct.** The author writes, "All other explanations for the war are either a direct consequence of the South's desire for wealth at the expense of her fellow man or a fanciful invention to cover up this sad portion of our nation's history."

34. **B) is correct.** The author writes, "The Civil War was not a battle of cultural identities—it was a battle about slavery. All other explanations for the war are either a direct consequence of the South's desire for wealth at the expense of her fellow man or a fanciful invention to cover up this sad portion of our nation's history."

35. **A) is correct.** The author writes, "But people who try to sell you this narrative are wrong. The Civil War was not a battle of cultural identities—it was a battle about slavery."

36. **C) is correct.** The passage describes human studies as the study of "the relationship between human activity and the environment," which would include farmers interacting with river systems.

37. **A) is correct.** The passage explains what the study of geography involves and outlines its main sub-disciplines.

38. **B) is correct.** Only this choice summarizes the two main points of the passage: the definition of geography and the breakdown of its sub-disciplines.

39. **C) is correct.** In the last paragraph the author writes, "Mammary glands are specialized examples of apocrine glands."

40. **B) is correct.** In the last paragraph the author writes, "Mammary glands are specialized examples of apocrine glands. Mammary glands produce milk following the birth of a child. Thus, sweat glands are not only associated with perspiration, but also lactation." Since this information will surprise most readers, readers can infer that it would surprise most other people, too.

41. **A) is correct.** The primary purpose of the passage is to inform; its focus is on types and functions of sweat glands. It is not persuasive. It does define the word *sweat*, but it covers more information than a simple definition.

42. **A) is correct.** The passage is mainly about the large number of American football players who develop CTE. The other sentences give details from the passage.

43. **C) is correct.** The passage does not contain this detail. The passage does not mention what stance professional football organizations are taking regarding CTE.

44. **A) is correct.** The author does not say whether studies on CTE among players have affected professional football one way or another. However, readers can infer that professional football's success may be threatened in the future, depending on public reaction to the studies.

45. **C) is correct.** In the second paragraph, the author writes, "Many concerned parents have begun to ask if football is too violent a sport for their children. It may be too early for Americans to honestly answer this question, but there is certainly room for growing concern."

46. **B) is correct.** In the first sentence, the author writes, "Chronic traumatic encephalopathy (CTE) is a degenerative brain disease that has garnered the attention of the media in recent years." The context shows that the author uses the phrase "garnered the attention of the media" to mean "gotten the attention of the news media."

47. **C) is correct.** In the first paragraph, the author points out that studies have shown that the vast majority of professional football players develop CTE, a serious brain illness. The second paragraph deals primarily with implications for younger athletes. The author writes, "Many concerned parents have begun to ask if football is too violent a sport for their children." The evidence in the passage suggests that the author may think that football is too violent for athletes of all ages.

48. **B) is correct.** The passage states that "infants rely primarily on hearing."

49. **A) is correct.** The passage explains how a baby's senses develop and allow it to interact with the world.

50. **C) is correct.** The passage states that babies' senses are much like those of their adult counterparts with the exception of their vision, which develops later.

51. **C) is correct.** The passage is mainly about the "troubling" fact that 40 million people in the United States still smoke, even though most people know that heavy smoking shortens people's lives. The other sentences give details from the passage.

52. **C) is correct.** In the last sentence, the author writes, "the United States still has a long road of anti-smoking campaigning ahead." Readers can infer that by "a long road" the author means "a lot of hard work left to do."

53. **A) is correct.** The author uses various phrases to describe the cause-effect relationship between cigarette smoking and serious illnesses. Other words and phrases the author uses include "link," "cigarette-linked cancers," "is linked to," and "correlated with."

54. **B) is correct.** The passage does not contain this detail. The passage does not mention advertising.

55. **A) is correct.** In the last paragraph, the author states that "[c]ontinuing research reinforces the necessity of anti-smoking campaigns, both government funded and grassroots. The numbers show that such campaigns work, encouraging people to quit smoking." Clearly, the author is strongly in favor of "anti-smoking campaigns."

56. **B) is correct.** Words and phrases such as "40 million people continue to smoke," "troubling," "30 percent of all cancer-related deaths in the United States can be tied to smoking," and "the necessity of anti-smoking campaigns" show that the author thinks all smokers should quit—the sooner the better.

57. **A) is correct.** The primary purpose of the essay is to inform; its focus is on the definition of empathy. It is not persuasive or advisory. The author does not set out to show that one quality is better than another.

58. **C) is correct.** In the last paragraph the author writes, "some people with very strong cognitive empathy may abuse their social understanding as a means to take advantage of others." Earlier the author defines "cognitive empathy" as "the ability to identify and understand the emotions, mental state, or perspective of others."

59. **A) is correct.** In the last paragraph, the author states, "Empathy is crucial for being able to respond properly in social settings." The reader can infer from this information that empathy is a positive quality that people need in order to treat others in a socially acceptable manner.

60. **B) is correct.** In the second paragraph, the author defines compassionate empathy as "the ability to control your own emotions while helping others deal with theirs." Readers can infer that this kind of empathy would be useful to medical professionals who have to remain calm in emergencies (when patients and bystanders are often upset).

Made in United States
Cleveland, OH
13 April 2025

16058370R00059